PRAISE FOR *THE JESUS I DIDN'T KNOW I DIDN'T KNOW*

"In this excellent work, Reddish skillfully walks the line between introductory primer and in-depth examination of the person of Jesus. I often found myself reflecting on new and astute insights I had not considered before. I highly recommend this book to those new to Christian studies, as well as to those who think they already know all there is to know about Jesus."

—Wm. Curtis Holtzen, Professor of Philosophy and Theology, Hope International University, and author of *The God Who Trusts*

"If you could draw together the best devotional writing and the best biblical scholarship and fuse them into a single book, then you would have *The Jesus I Didn't Know I Didn't Know*. Make no mistake, you will not be able to read these words and remain unchanged. Some of the chapters will move you, others will challenge you, and some will just plain knock you out! It's a complete heart, mind, and soul workout— and I can't recommend it highly enough."

—Nicholas Bundock, Rector of St James and Emmanuel Church, Manchester, United Kingdom

"This engaging biblical study helps us get a glimpse inside the minds and times of the gospel writers to embrace who Jesus really was and is, in the same way they did—through Jesus' revolutionary, startling, hope-giving statements, actions, and experiences. Reddish has mined fascinating insights that will provide rich fodder for individuals and groups, teachers, and preachers. If you think you already know all about Jesus, then read this book! It's fresh, friendly, and faith-building. Discover facets and nuances of the person and work of Jesus and what it means to follow him."

—Catherine Lawton, poet and author of *Glimpsing Glory*

"Tim Reddish writes like a learned friend. With writing precision, Tim navigates the space between learning and encouraging. I was persistently aware of the sense that I was listening to someone that cared about me; that he was unveiling for me previously unrealized, simple, but explosive ideas. Ideas with which I could both easily engage and understand... Tim presents a truth, and then, rather than overwhelm a reader, takes an example and unpacks it in a way that is accessible. I think that newcomers to faith and those long in the journey will benefit from reading this book."

—ROLAND HEARN, District Superintendent, Australia North and West District of the Church of the Nazarene, and Coordinator for Ministry in Australia and New Zealand

"The more I study the life of Jesus, the more I discover there are still many things to uncover. This isn't due to a lack of education or determination; it's just that as time goes by, I continually come across new insights. Tim Reddish understands that principle and offers us in *The Jesus I Didn't Know I Didn't Know* an introduction to the life of Jesus. He whets the appetite of the seeker of understanding concerning this person called Jesus as he invites us to join him on a journey of discovery of new truths concerning the life of Jesus."

—ROBERT D. CORNWALL, Pastor of Central Woodward Christian Church, Troy, Michigan, and author of numerous books, including *Unfettered Spirit*

The Jesus I Didn't Know
I Didn't Know

The Jesus I Didn't Know I Didn't Know

Reflections on the Identity of Jesus

TIM REDDISH

WIPF & STOCK · Eugene, Oregon

THE JESUS I DIDN'T KNOW I DIDN'T KNOW
Reflections on the Identity of Jesus

Copyright © 2021 Tim Reddish. All rights reserved. Except for brief quotations in critical publications or reviews, no part of this book may be reproduced in any manner without prior written permission from the publisher. Write: Permissions, Wipf and Stock Publishers, 199 W. 8th Ave., Suite 3, Eugene, OR 97401.

All scriptural references are from the New Revised Standard Version (NRSV) Bible translation, unless otherwise specified as from the New International Version (NIV) or the New English Translation (NET) Bible.

Scripture quoted by permission. Quotations designated NET are from the NET Bible® copyright ©1996, 2019 by Biblical Studies Press, L.L.C. http://netbible.com. All rights reserved.

Wipf & Stock
An Imprint of Wipf and Stock Publishers
199 W. 8th Ave., Suite 3
Eugene, OR 97401

www.wipfandstock.com

PAPERBACK ISBN: 978-1-6667-0877-6
HARDCOVER ISBN: 978-1-6667-0878-3
EBOOK ISBN: 978-1-6667-0879-0

06/24/21

This book is lovingly dedicated to
Mary Esther Reddish

What does Jesus mean to me? To me, he was one of the greatest teachers humanity has ever had.... Jesus was the most active resister known perhaps to history. His was nonviolence *par excellence*.

MAHATMA GANDHI

Jesus Christ was an extremist for love, truth, and goodness.... Jesus is not an impractical idealist; he is the practical realist.

MARTIN LUTHER KING JR.

Jesus was not a theologian. He was God who told stories.

MADELEINE L'ENGLE

I am a Jew, but I am enthralled by the luminous figure of the Nazarene .... No one can read the Gospels without feeling the actual presence of Jesus. His personality pulsates in every word. No myth is filled with such life.

ALBERT EINSTEIN

Jesus didn't limit his ministry to the four walls of the church. He was out there fighting injustice and speaking truth to power every single day. He was out there spreading a message of grace and redemption to the least, the last, and the lost. And our charge is to find him everywhere, every day by how we live our lives.

MICHELLE OBAMA

Jesus was the first socialist, the first to seek a better life for mankind.

MIKHAIL GORBACHEV

The final and full revelation of God is not a book, it is a person.
Jesus Christ.

DESMOND TUTU

Jesus is the most fascinating character in history, really—the character who's made more difference to the world than anyone since him . . .

PHILIP PULLMAN

Jesus was a Jew, and also I believe he was a catalyst, and I think he offended people because his message was to love your neighbor as yourself; in other words, no one is better than somebody else . . . . So he rattled a lot of people's cages.

MADONNA

When people say, you know, "good teacher," "prophet," "really nice guy" . . . this is not how Jesus thought of himself. So you're left with a challenge . . . which is either Jesus was who he said he was or he was a complete and utter nut case. You have to make a choice on that.

BONO

I believe Jesus Christ was the most courageous of persons because he dared to love.

MAYA ANGELOU

I've always considered Christ to be one of the greatest revolutionaries in the history of humanity.... I never saw a contradiction between the ideas that sustain me and the ideas of that symbol, of that extraordinary figure—Jesus Christ.

Fidel Castro

For Jesus, there are no countries to be conquered, no ideologies to be imposed, no people to be dominated. There are only children, women, and men to be loved.

Henri Nouwen

For me, the life of Jesus Christ . . . is an inspiration and an anchor in my life. A role-model of reconciliation and forgiveness; he stretched out his hands in love, acceptance, and healing. Christ's example has taught me to seek to respect and value all people of whatever faith or none.

Queen Elizabeth II

The love of God is not something vague or generic; the love of God has a name and a face: Jesus Christ.

Pope Francis

Contents

Preface		xv
Acknowledgments		xix
List of Abbreviations		xxi
Chapter 1	The Birth of Jesus	1
Chapter 2	The Baptism of Jesus	11
Chapter 3	The Temptation of Jesus	20
Chapter 4	The Titles of Jesus	28
Chapter 5	The Claims of Jesus	36
Chapter 6	The Politics of Jesus	53
Chapter 7	The Temple of Jesus	66
Chapter 8	The Supremacy of Jesus	74
Afterword		83
Bibliography		87
Other Books by Tim Reddish		91

Preface

You would think that I, being an ordained minister, should be an expert on Jesus. A modest expert anyway—not a true professional, like a genuine New Testament scholar! I mean, after all, I preach about Jesus week after week. I have been a minister for just over three years now, routinely preaching from the Gospels and following the liturgical calendar, and I am increasingly surprised by how much I didn't know about Jesus. That might shock you, so let me provide some background. I am sixty-one years old, and becoming a Presbyterian minister has been a second career, as it were. Prior to following this new calling on my life, I was a physics professor for nearly twenty-five years. Moreover, I have been a Christian since I was thirteen. My parents were missionaries, and I was educated at Christian boarding schools.[1] Throughout my adult life I have been actively following Jesus, including integrating my faith with science.[2] My first wife, Anne, and I were also intimately involved in leading home groups (Bible/book studies) in the various churches we attended over the years. My personal faith has also been tested and refined through suffering: Anne died from cancer in 2011 after a six-year battle with the disease.[3] I later resigned from my tenured professorship to study theology at Knox College, Toronto, and—upon graduation—I was

---

1. For the curious, I attended Hillcrest School in Jos, Nigeria, from 1969 to 1976 (in the class of 1977). From 1976 to 1978 I attended King Edward's School, Witley, United Kingdom, and was a leader in the Christian Union.
2. See Reddish, *Science and Christianity*.
3. See Reddish, *Does God Always Get What God Wants?*

Preface

awarded the Gold Medal for academic excellence. You might think that with this experience and training I should know a fair bit about Jesus! From my perspective, not enough.

Now, let me say at this point that *The Jesus I Didn't Know I Didn't Know* is not the result of a failure of my seminary professors at Knox. Everyone knows the curriculum typically encompasses a wide range of important material, and it is impossible to cover everything. You always learn on the job in ministry. Seminary teaches you how to teach yourself. It's all about life-long learning, right? Therefore, discovering the Jesus I didn't know I didn't know is a sign that my training was successful.

If you reflect on this a little, however, it's self-evident that it is healthy for a minister to be learning more about Jesus all the time and communicating those insights to others. And not just learning about Jesus, but endeavouring to integrate Jesus's message with all aspects of living and authentically modelling that behaviour. Christians would say that both of those elements are signs of the Holy Spirit at work in someone's life. If that were not happening, you would hopefully be concerned.

So precisely what about Jesus didn't I know I didn't know? Responding to that question is the purpose of this book. In brief, what I didn't realize is how much an underlying purpose of the Gospels is to reveal the *identity* of Jesus. Those who know the New Testament well will agree this is particularly evident in John's Gospel. However, we could dismiss his bold claims as just one voice—and a maverick one at that! Are John's claims about Jesus echoed in the other three Gospels: Matthew, Mark, and Luke?[4] And what about the Jesus of Paul and the other New Testament writers—is their portrayal of Jesus consistent with those of the Gospel writers? This book, then, reflects on the identity of Jesus through the eyes of various New Testament writers. I was surprised to find many claims about the person of Jesus outside of John's account that essentially affirm John's distinctive view of Jesus's identity.

While it is also true that there is a lot about Jesus I didn't know I didn't know concerning his teaching, miracles, and passion

---

4. They are known collectively as the Synoptic Gospels, as they are to be seen or viewed together.

Preface

(meaning the events of the last week of Jesus's life, notably his suffering), I will not be focusing on those aspects in this project. What I have discovered through studying the works of various authors has shocked me. It makes me wonder if I was really listening while attending church for fifty years! Or whether my ministers were inadvertently omitting—or, worse, withholding—important aspects of the Jesus story.

See what you think. . .

Acknowledgments

The material in this book arose out of a thematic selection from three years' worth of my weekly sermons, primarily from the Gospels, which were then heavily adapted. Preparation for those homilies naturally involved reading and research. Like a sponge, I absorbed information from various sources. In the process, as I said in the preface, what I discovered surprised me greatly. This work is, therefore, part original and part synthesis of what I have learned from studying the works of numerous scholars—as seen through my own theological and hermeneutical lenses. Like a magpie, I gathered information from various sources, and it is therefore not easy, or even possible, to recall the origins of all the snippets of wisdom I have gleaned on this journey. I do, however, know my regular go-to sources, and I want to freely acknowledge my use of that material in this work. In terms of Bible commentaries, I found the *New Interpreter's Bible Commentary* series to be most informative, counterbalanced by N. T. Wright's more popular *New Testament for Everyone* series. I particularly found the academic commentaries of Eugene Boring (on Matthew and Mark) to be most insightful. Furthermore, I benefitted greatly from the perceptiveness of the contributors in the *Feasting on the Word* lectionary series. And Richard B. Hays's *Echoes of Scripture in the Gospels* is simply a must-read to appreciate references (and allusions) to the Old Testament in the Gospels. Therefore, I especially thank all those authors and wholeheartedly recommend their works for further study, along with the other books listed in the bibliography.

Acknowledgments

I also acknowledge with gratitude Matthew Wimer, Mike Surber, my copyeditor Rebecca Abbott, and my typesetter Savanah Landerholm, along with the entire team at Wipf & Stock for bringing this project to fruition.

Naturally, I would like to thank my whole family for their continual love and support: Phil and Greer in Edmonton, along with our lively, growing grandchildren, Arthur, Beatrice, and Elliot; more locally, Adam, Andrew, Jonathan, and Julia—who, each in their own unique way, are all maturing so fast into remarkable adults! Finally, and most especially, to my wife Mary—to whom this book is dedicated—for your encouragement and patience on this amazing adventure that we share together.

Tim Reddish, Easter 2021

List of Abbreviations

LXX	The Septuagint, the Greek translation of the Hebrew Scriptures
NET	NET Bible
NIV	New International Version
NRSV	New Revised Standard Version
YHWH	Yahweh, the (unspoken) personal name for God in the Old Testament

Chapter 1

The Birth of Jesus

Only the Gospels of Matthew and Luke give us birth narratives for Jesus.[1] Put simply, Luke presents us with a perspective based on Mary, and Matthew gives us a viewpoint from Joseph. What we tend to do, especially at Christmastime, is to merge the two stories together. However, there is no evidence that Matthew and Luke knew of each other's accounts when they wrote them. The two stories do not fit together perfectly, because they were written for different audiences and with different purposes in mind.[2] I therefore think it's best to keep their narratives separate and take each one on its own merits. That way, it is straightforward to see how they each enhance their respective Gospels as a whole. I will simply consider Matthew's account here.

Many years ago, I was interested in tracing my family tree. This was before Ancestry.com and the power of the internet. It was all done laboriously by hand at the national records office and—needless to say—I soon tired of it. Matthew's Gospel begins with what seems to us to be a boring genealogy of Jesus.[3] Matthew traces Jesus's lineage back through David to Abraham, so emphasizing

---

1. See Matt 1:18—2:23 and Luke 1:26—2:52.

2. For example, Matthew has no journey from Nazareth to Bethlehem, as in Luke 2:4, and he first mentions Nazareth in Matt 2:23. Luke makes no mention of the escape to Egypt (see Matt 2:13–15; Luke 2:39).

3. Matt 1:1–17. The word translated "genealogy" means origin (1:1), and its Greek root (*genesis*) is repeated in 1:18.

The Jesus I Didn't Know I Didn't Know

to his Jewish readers that the birth of Jesus is part of the ongoing story of Israel. Furthermore, Matthew begins his Gospel by forthrightly stating that Jesus is the Messiah, the son of David,[4] but ends his genealogy in a rather peculiar way. Instead of his usual, "*This* person was the father of *that* person," he states, "Joseph [was] the husband of Mary, and Mary was the mother of Jesus who is called the Messiah."[5] Clearly there was some ambiguity as to who was the father of Mary's son. Everyone who read his account would have realized this oddity, and the next few verses are, perhaps, Matthew's way of trying to explain or clarify what he meant.[6]

I suspect that there were some rumors circulating concerning the birth of Jesus which were not very flattering towards Mary, suggesting some kind of sexual impropriety.[7] (Note: *no* disrespect is intended here.) Both Matthew and Luke's birth stories could therefore be seen as setting the record straight. Many have noticed Matthew's earlier mention of Tamar, Rahab, Ruth, and Bathsheba in his genealogy. Why are they there, when the matriarchs Sarah, Rebekah, and Leah are not? What is intriguing is that all these women are non-Jews, and therefore not only does this remind his readers of their faith and tenacity, but perhaps it's a hint that God's salvation would finally embrace those outside of the Jewish race. This seems perfectly justified in that Matthew then goes on to relate his story of the Magi—or wise men—from the East.[8] Some, however, have plausibly suggested that these women are mentioned in the context of various kinds of sexual misconduct or abuse and therefore act as a backdrop to the story of Jesus's mother, Mary, who was suspected of having had a scandalous sexual relationship.

---

4. Matt 1:1. His stress is on both titles, since he repeats twice more Messiah (in 1:17, 18) and son of David (in 1:20).

5. Matt 1:16 NIV. In Luke 3:23 NIV we read: "He [Jesus] was the son, *so it was thought*, of Joseph" (italics added).

6. See Matt 1:18–25.

7. Some scholars treat John 8:41 as a reference to Christ's (questionable) birth.

8. See Matt 2:1–12.

The Birth of Jesus

Matthew tells us that Mary was engaged to Joseph.[9] Marriages in those days were arranged by the parents, and this promise of marriage was legally as binding as being married. That is why Matthew uses the words "husband," "wife," and "divorce" in describing the nature of their relationship. The bride-to-be still lived in her father's house until the formal wedding ceremony. However, before Mary married Joseph and moved into his home, she was found to be pregnant, and Matthew explains to his readers that this was a work of the Holy Spirit.[10] Joseph hears about this pregnancy, knows he is not the father, and so has a crisis of conscience. He wants to do the right thing, but what should he do? We are told that Joseph was a "righteous man." This means he faithfully kept the Mosaic law and therefore knew precisely what he had to do. He had no choice: he must divorce her. No matter how much he loved Mary, it was his religious obligation to annul the marriage contract, because she was apparently guilty of having had sex before marriage. In earlier times, this was a crime punishable by death.[11] By the first century, there were other ways to annul the marriage. But this, of necessity, would still be public and therefore bring great shame to teenage Mary.[12] This, Matthew tells us, Joseph does not want to do. He wishes he could divorce Mary quietly, with no formal investigation into her behavior.[13] Balancing justice and mercy was, it appears, part of Joseph's crisis of conscience.

We are told God's messenger appears to him in a dream. This would make all Jewish readers remember the dreams of Joseph in the Old Testament—you know, the one with the technicolor dreamcoat! The angel says, "Joseph son of David, do not be afraid to take Mary home as your wife, because what is conceived in her is from the Holy Spirit."[14] We quickly learn three things here: first, it is Joseph, not Mary, who is descended from David, and so there

---

9. Matt 1:18.
10. Matt 1:18.
11. Deut 22:23–24.
12. Culturally, it is generally considered that Mary was most likely a young teenager at the time.
13. Matt 1:19.
14. Matt 1:20b NIV.

is an issue of how the future child will be considered part of David's lineage—given Joseph is not the father. Second, Mary is still living in her parents' home at this time. And third, Joseph is now informed of what Matthew told his readers earlier, namely, the child's conception is "from the Holy Spirit." What that means I will discuss in a moment. The angel then says, "She [Mary] will give birth to a son, and you are to give him the name Jesus, because he will save his people from their sins."[15] This message, then, contains some kind of explanation for Mary's pregnancy which, strange as it may seem, was meant to reassure Joseph. In addition, it gives two instructions: go ahead with the marriage, and name the son Jesus. Matthew later tells us that Joseph did just that.[16]

Matthew then inserts his own commentary into the events, one that was no doubt meant as an added explanation of the angel's message. He writes,

> All this took place to fulfill what the LORD had said through the prophet: "The virgin will conceive and give birth to a son, and they will call him Immanuel" (which means "God with us").[17]

This verse has generated a life of its own within church history, one Matthew likely did not intend, and so we come to the Christian doctrine of the virgin birth—one that we recite in our traditional creeds.[18] Let's pause and explore this aspect briefly.

The trouble with this verse is that we fix our attention on the word virgin and get side-tracked into sexual status and biology, whereas Matthew presumably wanted us to see God's action in

---

15. Matt 1:21 NIV.

16. Matt 1:24–25. And Matthew adds that Joseph did not have sex with Mary until after Jesus was born.

17. Matt 1:22–23 NIV; Matthew cites (and adapts) Isa 7:14. This is the *only* citation of Isa 7:14 in the New Testament. Matthew repeatedly stresses Jesus as *fulfilling* the Scriptures. This is a feature of his persuasive rhetoric to help convince skeptical Jews that Jesus was indeed the long-awaited Messiah. See Matt 2:6, 15–18, 23; 3:3; 8:17; 11:10; 12:17–21; 15:7–9; 21:4–5, 42; 27:9–10.

18. Virgin birth is a misnomer; virgin conception is meant. Moreover, Mary had other children; Jesus had siblings. See Matt 13:55–56; Mark 6:3; John 2:12; Gal 1:19.

The Birth of Jesus

history and the identity of Jesus. First, there is no evidence that first-century Jews had an expectation that the messiah's birth must arise from a miraculous conception. Matthew's account would therefore have surprised Jews too.[19] Yes, Matthew quotes Isa 7:14 from the popular Greek LXX translation of the Old Testament, which has the word virgin, but the earlier Hebrew original uses instead the words "young woman," so there is evidently some linguistic ambiguity here.[20] This subtle difference may be disconcerting or perplexing, so let's have a short detour and consider Isa 7:14. Bear with me here, I think the diversion is worth it.

Isaiah was writing around 735 BCE during the reign of King Ahaz of Judah, also known as the Southern Kingdom, at a time of war.[21] King Pekah of Israel (or the Northern Kingdom, whose capital was Samaria) attacked King Ahaz in Jerusalem, but could not take the city, so he besieged it.[22] King Pekah then allied himself with King Rezin of Syria,[23] which caused great fear in the heart of King Ahaz and his people. God told Isaiah to advise and reassure King Ahaz,[24] but the king's response demonstrates his unwillingness to trust in God.[25] Isaiah then tells Ahaz that God will give him a gracious sign of confirmation: "Look, the young woman is with child and shall bear a son, and shall name him Immanuel."[26] The woman is most likely Abi(jah), the wife of the king, and having a son was a reassuring sign of the continuity of the Davidic line. Their

---

19. It therefore appears as though Matthew found the verse (Isa 7:14) *because* he knew of the Mary's unusual story!

20. See Isa 7:14 NRSV, NET. The familiar word "virgin" (from the Greek LXX, also known as the Septuagint) is cited in Matt 1:23 and Luke 1:27, 34—and is implied in Matt 1:18, 20, 25.

21. The Syro-Ephraimite war (735–732 BCE), see 2 Kgs 15:29—16:20 and 2 Chr 28. This was well before the Babylonian exile.

22. Isa 7:1; 2 Kgs 16:5.

23. Or Aram, with its capital in Damascus.

24. Isa 7:3–9.

25. Isa 7:12–13.

26. Isa 7:14 NRSV; cf. NET, NIV. See too the connection between Immanuel, meaning "God with us," and "the Lord is with you" in the call of Gideon (Judg 6:12, 16). In other words, this kind of language need not be restricted to a messianic interpretation.

The Jesus I Didn't Know I Didn't Know

son, Hezekiah, was later born and Isa 9:2–7 is usually understood as a song of celebration at his birth.[27] You might be familiar with those words too: "For a child *has been* born for us, a son given to us; authority rests upon his shoulders; and he is named Wonderful Counselor, Mighty God, Everlasting Father, Prince of Peace."[28] These grand titles suggest a profound belief in God's provision of this child and of God's involvement in history. Christians typically interpret these proclamations as messianic prophecies that were fulfilled in Jesus. I share that view. However, Isa 7:14 and 9:2–7 *also* had an *immediate* context and fulfilment in the minds of Isaiah and his audience. This historical background is, I believe, important and often overlooked. It is Matthew himself (not the angel) who makes the connection with Isa 7:14, and he—curiously—cites the Greek LXX rather than the Hebrew version. One could understand his point this way: just as God provided a sign confirming God was proactive in Isaiah's situation, so God is doing the same again in Matthew's day through the birth of Jesus. God is palpably with us!

It must also be remembered that miraculous birth stories are typically a sign that God is powerfully at work. Consider the births of John the Baptist to Elizabeth, Samuel to Hannah, and Isaac to Sarah, Jacob and Esau—twins, a double blessing—to Rebekah.[29] Furthermore, to speak of the conception of Jesus as a work of the Holy Spirit is to say that this is an *inexplicable, creative* act of the divine spirit—and that distinction from God the Father is significant.

---

27. Or Hezekiah's coronation (or a combination of both). Isa 9:2–7 is a hymn of thanksgiving rather than a prophecy. Prophecy needs to be understood more in terms of *forth-telling* than in *foretelling*, and a community of faith can believe such oracles to have more than one meaning. See, for example, Isa 40:1–11, esp. 3; Matt 3:3; Mark 1:2–3; Luke 3:4–6; John 1:23.

28. Isa 9:6; italics added. These words are well-known from Handel's *Messiah*. Notice the past verb tense implies a fulfilment. This could, however, be seen as the prophetic past, where the events are still in the future but are put in the past tense as they are as good as done. See *Jewish Study Bible*, 801.

29. See Luke 1; 1 Sam 1; and Gen 21:1–6; 25:21. Like Sarah, Elizabeth was childless and was considered too old to conceive (Luke 1:7). In the case of Sarah, the language of "conception is of the Holy Spirit" seems to be echoed in Jubilees 16:12, "And . . . the LORD visited Sarah and did unto her as He had spoken and she conceived."

The Birth of Jesus

So, a miraculous conception is not concerned with nature as such, though it does impinge on the process of conception, but, much more importantly, it identifies those persons as having a special role in God's historical drama of saving God's people.[30]

Moving on, we have to be careful not to say that the virgin conception is central to the Christian claim that Jesus is divine (as well as human). That would, in my view, be an unwise attempt to force later trinitarian thinking into the birth narratives. Think about that for a moment. Are Christians claiming that Mary was somehow (and we certainly can't know how!) impregnated by God, and consequently her child was both human and divine? This is problematic, because to have one divine parent and one human parent is not what Christians mean by incarnation, or God enfleshed. The very literal—and unsatisfactory—interpretation of that notion results in Jesus being a hybrid, a demigod, half-human and half-divine—not fully human and not fully divine, as Christians believe him to be! No, the traditional belief in the divinity of Jesus the Messiah is based on faith in more subtle indicators of the uniqueness of Jesus, as we will see later, and not merely in some stand-alone, unspecified, biological explanation. Moreover, Mark, John, and Paul make absolutely no reference to a virgin conception—and they would have, if they had thought this was important in establishing Christ's identity.[31] And Matthew, having mentioned it, doesn't base any subsequent theology on this miracle. That being the case, let's follow their example.

Instead of focusing on Mary, it seems to me Matthew's attention is on *who* this baby is and *what* he will do. Matthew is emphatic:

---

30. Consider too Moses's birth story, Exod 2:1–10. In Jesus's day there were also stories that Moses's birth was supernatural. Even so, Isaac, Moses, and Samuel were *not* seen as a divine; rather, they each had a special role in God's salvation history.

31. See John 1:1–18 (whose Gospel is widely regarded as having the highest Christology) and Rom 1:1–7, where Paul stresses the resurrection (v. 4)—rather than the birth (v. 3)—of Jesus. More generally, Paul's scandalous message was *not* of Christ's birth, but of him *crucified*, which was considered shameful and offensive to Jews. Moreover, death by crucifixion meant that the person was deemed a rebel or a criminal and so, for non-Jews, Jesus was not a credible person to follow. See 1 Cor 1:18–25.

The Jesus I Didn't Know I Didn't Know

Jesus is the Messiah,[32] and, as the angel said, this child is different for "he will save his people from their sins."[33] And the rest of Matthew's Gospel relates how that will come about. Incidentally, the name Jesus has the same root as the name Joshua, meaning "God (YHWH) is salvation," and was a popular boy's name at the time. Joshua was, of course, the successor to Moses,[34] and a key theme of Matthew is Jesus fulfilling a Moses-like role.[35] Moreover, Matthew, by citing Isaiah, identifies Jesus with Immanuel, "God with us."[36] All this is a sign to Matthew's readers as to who he thinks Jesus is and what he will do.

Now what about that genealogical problem I mentioned earlier concerning Jesus being a "son of David"? In obedience to the angel, Joseph names the child Jesus.[37] The action of a man naming the child makes the child legally his own.[38] Joseph's naming of Jesus results in him having all the legal rights of sonship, including inheritance and lineage. Jesus is therefore considered an authentic descendant of King David.

Before finishing this chapter, it is worth a brief digression concerning divine messengers. We are puzzled as to what to make of angelic beings; we find angels quaint in a nativity play, but we are not sure if we really believe in their existence. I am not, obviously, talking about the stereotypical portrayal of angels dressed in white

---

32. Matt 1:1, 17, 18. This triple emphasis in the opening chapter leaves no ambiguity for Matthew or his readers.

33. Matt 1:21b.

34. Num 27:12–23; Deut 31:7–23; Josh 1:5–9. It was Joshua who led the Israelites across the River Jordan into the Promised Land.

35. For example, the Sermon on the Mount (Matt 5–7) mirrors Moses on Mt. Sinai giving the law to the people.

36. "God with us" does not have to be seen as a high Christology; see also page 5, footnote 26. His name is simply a sign (Isa 7:14). Jews did not think the messiah was a divine figure. However, at the end of Matthew's Gospel we do have a high Christology, see Matt 28:18–20. And there are also other hints along the way; see Matt 10:40; 18:20; 24:35 (Isa 40:8); 25:40 (Prov 19:17).

37. Matt 1:25b.

38. More generally in Jewish culture, the child's mother was not in doubt, only his paternity. For the *father* to name him is therefore significant in terms of formally adopting the child.

The Birth of Jesus

and with wings, but rather the notion of a divine messenger in a humanlike form. Whatever we may think, the Bible contains various accounts of angels, and it would be unwise to simply dismiss their presence. It seems to me that it is the *message* attributed to angels that is critically important; that's where we should focus our attention. Since the Gospel writers are claiming the angels' messages have a divine origin, we consequently expect their contents to be: (a) truthful, therefore reliable information, and (b) something one could not deduce by human reason—a revelation. (Incidentally, the same can be said about visions.[39]) In a way, the message's function is to convey to the recipient(s) some special news, information that may need to be promptly acted upon. Moreover, it alerts the reader that the veracity of the message will be demonstrated by the end of the Gospel, so authenticating the message and making plain its divine origin. For example, the angel says to Joseph, "She [Mary] will give birth to a son," which she does,[40] and "he [Jesus] will save his people from their sins,"[41] and how that comes about is presented in the rest of Matthew's Gospel. In Luke's Gospel, the angel tells Zechariah that his childless wife, Elizabeth, will have a son (John the Baptist) and then explains his specific role in God's story of salvation. (We will consider that role in the next chapter.) In the same way, the angel Gabriel tells Mary,

> He [Jesus] will be great and will be called the Son of the Most High. The Lord God will give him the throne of his father David, and he will reign over Jacob's descendants forever; his kingdom will never end.[42]

In all three situations, the messenger reveals crucial theological information that we would not be able deduce from reason alone, and the reader then expects to see this realized. This conclusion

---

39. See Matt 2:12, 19–20. Furthermore, angels and visions are not unique to the Judeo-Christian tradition.

40. The point being the child could have been a girl, but was not. This is evidence that the first part of the message was true.

41. Matt 1:21 NIV.

42. Luke 1:32–33 NIV. Consider too the angel's message to the shepherds in Luke 2:9–12.

The Jesus I Didn't Know I Didn't Know

is one of those things I didn't know I didn't know. It significantly alters the way we typically understand these birth narratives and, consequently, influences how we approach the rest of the Gospels of Matthew and Luke.

Chapter 2

The Baptism of Jesus

The baptism of Jesus is thought to have occurred about thirty years after his birth. The church traditionally celebrates Jesus's baptism early in the new year during the season of Epiphany. Epiphany means revelation or manifestation—a (divine) mystery being made plain. Consequently, in the baptism of Jesus something special is being revealed. But what exactly is it?

Mark's Gospel, which was the first of the four Gospels to be written, says, "John the baptizer appeared in the wilderness, proclaiming a baptism of repentance for the forgiveness of sins."[1] Matthew was fully aware of Mark's account when he wrote his own, and he includes and edits Mark's material, expanding it with information from other available sources. Matthew tells us that John's basic message was "repent, for the kingdom of heaven has come near."[2] (We will consider more of what that means in chapter 6.) He then adds that people came to John from all over the land to the River Jordan, and, "confessing their sins, they were baptized by him."[3] The interesting thing here is that Matthew does not link John's baptism with forgiveness, only repentance—and that's an important distinction. For Jews at that time, only God could forgive sins, and that

---

1. Mark 1:4. See Luke 3:3 for a similar declaration to Mark; nevertheless, see also Acts 19:3-4.

2. Matt 3:2.

3. Matt 3:5-6 NIV. Later Matthew has John the Baptist say explicitly, "I baptize you with water *for repentance*," Matt 3:11a (italics added).

The Jesus I Didn't Know I Didn't Know

was through sacrifices at the temple in Jerusalem. In fact, Jesus, just prior to his healing of a paralyzed man, was later accused of blasphemy by some religious leaders for claiming to be able to forgive sins.[4] At the end of his Gospel, Matthew explicitly links forgiveness with the crucifixion, using the words of Jesus at the Last Supper. It was there that Jesus instituted the practice of Holy Communion saying: "Drink from [this cup], all of you; for this is my blood of the covenant, which is poured out for many *for the forgiveness of sins*."[5] It seems clear, then, that for Matthew at least, John's baptism—a distinctive ritual cleansing—was only about repentance. And before we explore what that word means, let's pause to ascertain John's authority for what he was doing. Why? Because one thing I didn't know I didn't know was the importance of *authority* as a general theme within the Gospels—indeed, the whole of the New Testament.

Matthew indicates that John was a prophet, in other words, a person who was widely recognized to be holy and publicly acclaimed to be a divinely inspired messenger for a specific time and purpose. The other Gospel writers agree. This was a surprise in itself, because the Jews at that time had not experienced a prophet for several hundred years. Perhaps that's one explanation for the people's fascination with John and why they were willing to travel from the cities to the wilderness to hear him. While the religious elite may not have liked John's blunt message, they didn't openly deny that he was a prophet or denounce his baptism in the River Jordan.[6] John's authority, then, came primarily from the *people*, in that it was they who discerned John to be a prophet. Having said that, Luke—uniquely—provides a birth narrative for John.[7] John's parents both had eminent priestly pedigrees. Again, an angelic messenger was involved, and there was also a miraculous element to his

---

4. See Matt 9:1–8; Mark 2:5–12; Luke 5:17–26.

5. Matt 26:27–28 (italics added). This subtly links the death of Jesus with the Jewish practice of sacrifice.

6. See Matt 21:23–27. John the Baptist was calling the nation to repent, not just individuals. And using the River Jordan, as well as John's ministry being in the wilderness, are both highly symbolic/significant for Jews.

7. Luke 1:5–25.

The Baptism of Jesus

birth. Those aspects alone serve as a sign of John being special—from conception. Luke's birth story, then, flags John as a person to watch out for, with the expectation that his life's mission would be of great importance to God. This is what the divine messenger proclaims to John's father, Zechariah:

> [John] will be great in the sight of the Lord. He must never drink wine or strong drink; *even before his birth he will be filled with the Holy Spirit. He will turn many of the people of Israel to the Lord their God.* With *the spirit and power of Elijah* he will go before him . . . *to make ready a people prepared for the Lord.*[8]

For Luke, then, John's authority comes from *God*, and the angelic message spells out his divinely mandated role. All the Gospel writers indicate this oracle was fulfilled by John as an adult.

Repentance means a U-turn, a reorientation of one's life back to following God. It is more than confession, in that repentance is a call to think (and behave) differently. The people who responded to that call, and who were baptized by John, are the "many" the angel said he would bring back to the authentic worship of "the Lord their God." Furthermore, in Malachi, the last book of the Old Testament, we read a divine oracle saying, "I will send you the prophet Elijah before that great and terrible Day of the LORD comes."[9] Obviously, this is not the original Elijah coming back to earth.[10] But this tells us that an Elijah figure, a holy prophet of great stature, was anticipated by Jews and was understood to have the role of preparing "the way of the LORD."[11] And that LORD—according to the

---

8. Luke 1:15–17 (italics added). There are hints here that John would be dedicated to God from birth in the form of a Nazarite vow (cf. Luke 1:15; Num 6:1–21; Judg 13:2–5).

9. Mal 4:5; 3:1. The meaning of the Day of the LORD will be discussed in chapter 6.

10. According to 2 Kgs 2, Elijah did not die but went directly to heaven in a chariot of fire.

11. See Matt 3:3 (citing Isa 40:3), and here Matthew cites Mark verbatim (Mark 1:2–3). See also Luke 3:4–6; John 1:23. Note that LORD (YHWH) in Isa 40:3 becomes Lord (Greek: *kyrios*) in these Gospel texts; this may have significance. Consider, for example, the possible connection with Matt

13

The Jesus I Didn't Know I Didn't Know

New Testament—is Jesus, God's Chosen One, the Messiah. Now, in none of the Gospels does John the Baptist actually say that Jesus is the Messiah.[12] However, Matthew has already repeatedly told his readers that information.[13] And John the Baptist doesn't claim to be that Elijah figure either, but Matthew later tells us that Jesus himself identifies John the Baptist as that Elijah.[14] And as we have just seen above, Luke has an *angelic* messenger link John with Elijah.

Matthew also contrasts John's mission with that of "the One who is to come," who will baptize with the Holy Spirit.[15] We are then told that one day Jesus comes to the River Jordan to be baptized by John. But John tries to deter him, saying, "I need to be baptized by you, and yet you come to me?"[16] Matthew is the only Gospel writer to try to explain why it was necessary for Jesus to be baptized. Perhaps it was a question that he was often asked. It is, after all, an intriguing question! Christians today tend to think of the problem in terms of Jesus being sinless, and so there was nothing to forgive. But as mentioned earlier, Matthew's understanding of John's baptism was not in terms of forgiveness, simply of repentance. I think a better approach is to say that, given Jesus is the

---

1:23—Immanuel, "God with us." The title Lord will be discussed in chapter 4.

12. Although Matthew's account of the conversation between John the Baptist and Jesus just prior to his baptism assumes it. See Matt 3:13–15.

13. See Matt 1:1, 17, 18 (and implied in 2:4). Mark 1:1 also announces Jesus as Messiah to his readers, and Luke has an angel announce that information in Luke 2:11.

14. Matt 11:11–15 and Mark 1:6; 9:11–13 implies it, and Matthew reiterates and makes it explicit in 17:12–13. Moreover, Matthew repeatedly compares and contrasts John with Jesus: Matt 3:2/4:17; 3:5/4:23; 3:7/23:33. Incidentally, Mark mentions that "John was clothed with camel's hair, with a leather belt around his waist" (Mark 1:6, and Matthew cites it in Matt 3:4). This is not a throwaway statement on John's eccentric habits, but rather John wore clothes similar to Elijah (see 2 Kgs 1:8). Curiously, however, John the Baptist denies being Elijah in John 1:21, yet he identifies himself as the one referenced in Isa 40:3 in John 1:23. (Note: the fourth—or John's—Gospel was *not* written by John the Baptist.)

15. Matt 3:11–12; see also Luke 3:16–17. Both writers add "and fire," which indicates judgment. Mark and John omit the reference to fire (see Mark 1:8; John 1:33b). For more on baptism in the Holy Spirit, see Acts 2.

16. Matt 3:13–14 NET.

The Baptism of Jesus

Messiah—the One who is to come—it does make more sense that *he* should be baptizing John and not the other way around. However, that is not what happens; Jesus somehow persuades John to baptize him. I suggest this signifies a public act of submission and obedience to God, rather than the U-turn of repentance. Moreover, Jesus is expressing his solidarity with the people he came to save and not with the religious elite who didn't think they needed to repent. And Matthew's readers already know Christ's mission is to "save his people from their sins," because that is what the angel told a troubled Joseph earlier.[17] As mentioned at the end of the previous chapter, the use of a divine messenger to give that news means we can therefore be confident that God is going to fulfil God's own purposes and that divine promises have not been forgotten. The rest of the Gospel will tell us how all this works out. But it begins with Jesus humbly identifying himself with God's people, sharing in their life and ultimately dying for them. We have no idea if Jesus himself knew of his identity at the time. But we do know that as he submits to God through the action of baptism, something dramatic happens. Mark describes it this way:

> Just as Jesus was coming up out of the water, he saw heaven being torn open and the Spirit descending on him like a dove. And a voice came from heaven: "You are my Son, whom I love; with you I am well pleased."[18]

First, Jesus sees the heavens in the process of being ripped apart. The wording implies this was an act of God, and the same Greek verb is used of the temple curtain that was torn in two from top to bottom when Jesus died.[19] In both cases what had been sealed was suddenly flung open; what had been hidden was revealed. In addition, at the end of the dramatic opening chapter of John's Gospel, Jesus says to Nathanael, "Very truly I tell you [all], you will see heaven opened and the angels of God ascending and descending on

---

17. Matt 1:21.
18. Mark 1:10–11 NIV. Matt 3:16–17 and Luke 3:21–22 are less dramatic ("heaven was opened"), but the divine link ("heaven") is still clear.
19. See Mark 15:38.

The Jesus I Didn't Know I Didn't Know

the Son of Man."[20] All this imagery is reminiscent of Isa 64:1, "O that you would tear open the heavens and come down." This language not only speaks of prophetic hopes being fulfilled, but its wording even provides seed for the future doctrine of the incarnation: God himself coming in human form. The heavens being ripped open, then, implies this particular baptism is an event of cosmic significance and shows that the veiled mystery of God has now been made manifest and freely available. What an amazing epiphany! The noted theologian Karl Barth puts it this way: "It is astonishing to claim that God does not remain hidden in the heights of heaven, but descends to the depths of earthly life in order to be seen and heard by finite creatures."[21] This shocking claim is the essence of all the Gospel writers. Like the vision of Jacob's ladder,[22] it presents a picture in which God is not distant or disinterested, but close by. God is busy and active; it is just that God is hidden from our sight. The "heavens tearing apart," then, allows us to catch a glimpse into the very workings of what God wants to do in the world through Jesus.

Second, there is a sign of God's empowering Spirit coming upon Jesus "like a dove."[23] This indicates that God's coming judgement will not be achieved through a merciless or vengeful spirit, but by making peace. (John the Baptist understood, just like many Jews of the day did, that the messiah would come as a judge.) This description of dove-like may seem a passing comment, but it actually gives us a (surprising) hint of the kind of messiah Jesus would become. But this expression should not take the focus away from the Holy Spirit descending on him. While this is a vivid portrait of God's endorsement of Jesus, such happenings were not unique. In the Old Testament, key prophets and leaders encountered God in various dramatic ways as part of their authenticating call narratives.[24] The Holy Spirit's descent on Jesus and "remaining/alighting

---

20. John 1:51, citing Gen 28:12. The meaning of Son of Man will be discussed in chapter 4.
21. Cited in Bartlett and Taylor, eds., *Feasting on the Word* (Year B), 1:238.
22. See Gen 28:10–19.
23. Mark 1:10; Matt 3:16; Luke 3:22; John 1:32. See also Isa 11:1–2; 42:1.
24. See Exod 3:1—4:17; Judg 6:11–40; 1 Sam 3:1–21; Jer 1:4–10; Ezek 1:1—3:11; Isa 6:1–13; 40:1–11.

The Baptism of Jesus

on him"[25] signifies that Jesus is an authorized prophet. But what happens next points to something more . . .

Third, all this is accompanied by a divine voice from heaven saying, "This is my Son, the Beloved, with whom I am well pleased."[26] The voice from heaven affirms that Jesus is radically different. John the Baptist continues in the line of prophets in the pattern of Elijah, but Jesus is of another order of greatness. He is the beloved Son of God whose relationship with the Father is unique. This proclamation echoes the words from Isaiah that refer to the suffering servant of God: "Here is my servant, whom I uphold, my chosen, in whom my soul delights; I have put my spirit upon him; he will bring forth justice to the nations."[27] Citing a verse like this is not an isolated prooftext to make a point; rather, it points to a whole passage containing a relevant theme for the readers to recall—as Matthew later makes explicit.[28] Moreover, that public affirmation from heaven is reminiscent of words from the psalmist: "He said to me, 'You are my son; today I have begotten you,'"[29] which originally referred to a Davidic king and could be reinterpreted as messianic. Since Mark's Gospel does not have a birth narrative and instead begins with the baptism of Jesus, this event is central for understanding the rest of his Gospel, which is—above all—the story of Jesus and what God did through him.

Before moving on, it is worth commenting on the differences in how the Gospels begin. As just mentioned, Mark—whose Gospel was written first—announces to his readers in the very first verse that "Jesus is the Messiah, the Son of God,"[30] and then quickly follows up with the account of Jesus's baptism. Since messiah means "anointed one," the baptism account—with its voice from heaven and the coming of the Holy Spirit upon Jesus—reveals to Mark's readers *how* Jesus became God's Anointed One. Mark tells us that

---

25. John 1:32; Matt 3:16.

26. Matt 3:17. Mark 1:10–11 gives the impression that the words from heaven were heard only by Jesus (cf. John 1:32–33).

27. Isa 42:1.

28. See Matt 12:17–21, where he cites Isa 42:1–4.

29. Ps 2:7.

30. Mark 1:1 NIV.

The Jesus I Didn't Know I Didn't Know

subsequent to Jesus's baptism was a *divine* anointing—not something bestowed by John the Baptist—so authenticating all that follows in the Gospel.

A question that we often ask is, "Did Jesus know he was the Messiah?" If we believe in the historicity of the baptism account—and I do—then the answer must be yes. But I suspect that doesn't mean Jesus knew precisely what that would entail; this would be something he would discover along the way. Note, however, that this is quite a different question from, "Did Jesus know he was divine?" (We will consider the meaning of Son of God in chapter 4.) Too often we ask such questions from a trinitarian perspective, a doctrine in which I also believe but which was developed later. As part of that doctrine, Christians believe Jesus was fully God and fully human. The seeds of such majestic ideas are present in the New Testament, as we will see, but it is not wise or helpful to project them back into the mind of Jesus. We cannot really answer the question, "Who did Jesus think he was?" That is because Jesus didn't leave any authored documents on which to base a response. (Paul, on the other hand, wrote various letters, and so it is appropriate to ask: "Who did Paul think he was?" And Pauline scholars eagerly respond to that question!) The Gospel writers, each in their own way, address the "Who is Jesus?" question. This is the critical question to ask—and respond to—in light of his resurrection.[31] Clearly, the Gospel writers were all convinced he was Israel's long-awaited Messiah; even so, they present Jesus's identity in different ways.

Another question to ask is, "*When* did Jesus realize he was the Messiah?" It is not unreasonable to say that Mark understood this to have occurred just after Jesus's baptism. Moreover, in light of Ps 2:7, this event could be construed as God adopting Jesus as God's own son. Matthew and Luke had Mark's Gospel (or something very like it) before them when they wrote their own accounts. Perhaps, they added their birth narratives to correct what they thought might be a potential misunderstanding that could have arisen from Mark's account. Regardless, one way to understand the rationale for

---

31. Consider too the disciples' question in Matt 8:27 NIV: "What kind of man is this? Even the winds and the waves obey him!" See also Mark 4:41; Luke 8:25.

The Baptism of Jesus

their two different birth narratives is to say they both understood Jesus to be the Messiah *from his conception* onwards, which itself was a mysterious work of the Holy Spirit.[32] Jesus's baptism was, therefore, from their perspectives, a commissioning for mininstry and a public affirmation of what Mary and Joseph (and at least a few others) knew from the very beginning. More explicitly, Luke's peculiar account of Jesus going to the temple when he was twelve years old gives the reader the impression that a precocious Jesus knew who he was, or at least that his life was somehow special (say, as a prophet), even at that stage—long before his baptism.[33]

John's Gospel was the last to be written and can be additionally understood as a theological commentary on the life of Jesus. Curiously, John does not provide a birth narrative for Jesus, nor does he describe the details of Jesus's baptism. Instead, in some of the most breathtaking language in the Bible, he says the unique relationship between Jesus and God began *before* the creation of the world![34]

---

32. As mentioned in the previous chapter, it is important to note that both Matthew and Luke present the Holy Spirit's involvement in the birth of Jesus through a divine messenger (Matt 1:20–21; Luke 1:30–38, esp. 35). And both present subsequent, independent corroboration of Jesus' uniqueness through the visit of the Magi (Matt 2:1–12), the angelic message to the shepherds (Luke 2:10–14), and the encounter with Simeon (Luke 2:25–35). Angels, dreams, visions, and prophetic utterances are all indicative of God's involvement in the birth of Jesus. It is also important to recognize that birth narratives as a literary genre are significant in their own right; great people must have had remarkable birth stories! This was widely understood in the Jewish Scriptures, as well as in the Greco-Roman literature. Consider Moses, for example, and his birth story (Exod 2:1–10), and the miracle of the birth of Samuel (1 Sam 1:1—2:21). These are paralleled in Matthew (Moses) and Luke (Samuel); the latter links the songs of Hannah, Elizabeth, and Mary and their three miraculous conceptions of sons, each of whom would have a significant role to play in salvation history.

33. See Luke 2:41–52, esp. 49–52.

34. See John 1:1–5, 14. This will be discussed in chapters 4 and 8.

Chapter 3

The Temptation of Jesus

Matthew tells us that, after Jesus's baptism, Jesus is *"led by the Spirit* into the wilderness *to be* tempted by the devil."[1] This is a scary thought if we take it literally, and we have to ask, "Is it true that God deliberately puts us into tough situations to test us?"[2] Personally, I don't think so—though you often hear people say such things. Yes, life can be very hard, and circumstances do test our character and faith, but I do not think God intentionally tests us just to see if we will trip up. Having said that, it is quite possible Matthew and his primarily Jewish audience *did* believe God was testing Jesus for reasons that will become clear in a moment. What Matthew says is even more disturbing, however, because the text could imply that God is collaborating with the devil.[3] Thankfully, Matthew later

---

1. Matt 4:1 (italics added). Note the Greek word for "test" is the same as "tempt," and some scholars say the better translation is test. Moreover, compare the wording with Mark 1:12–13 and Luke 4:1–2. They express it differently, giving the impression that God's Spirit led Jesus into the wilderness where he *happened* to be tested or tempted by the devil.

2. On this point see also Jas 1:12–15 (esp. 13). Note, however, there are key Old Testament stories of God testing people, such as Abraham (Gen 22:1–18) and the story of Job. This account is therefore in keeping with such Jewish traditions.

3. It could well be that Matthew is using/evoking the literary language of Job 1:6–12; 2:1–6. However, I question whether the image of Satan as the accuser wandering freely in the heavenly court is still appropriate for the New Testament, where the devil is portrayed as one who generally lies, deceives, and even attacks (e.g., John 8:44; 2 Thess 2:9–10; 1 Pet 5:8).

The Temptation of Jesus

gives the impression that God is, at best, tolerating the devil for the time being—and that might at least give us some reassurance![4]

Others find the mere mention of the devil or Satan too much to take seriously. Not least because to exclaim "The devil made me do it" is an escape from personal responsibility. I totally get it. However, even if we take "d" out of "devil," we still end up with a four-letter word! And that word evil itself is still problematic to many in Western society. Let me say, briefly, that I believe evil—a term that is admittedly tricky to define—is a reality greater than the sum of all our human inclination for wickedness. It is a power that holds the whole world in bondage and from which we need divine rescue. There are systemic evils, such as racism, greed, rampant consumerism, and ideologies that actively promote lies or violence—even resulting in genocide. And there are personal addictions, like gambling, alcohol, drugs, and pornography, as well as phobias, etc., that hold individuals in captivity. More generally, evil actively opposes the reign of God. In the New Testament, this dark force is given a face in the devil.[5] I suggest we don't get sidetracked by such personal representations of the undeniable experiential reality of evil. Instead, let's engage in the deeper significance of the story.

We are told that after having fasted forty days and forty nights in the wilderness, Jesus is hungry.[6] A good Jew would pick up on the mention of forty days and nights and immediately go back to Moses who also fasted for the same duration before God gave him the Ten Commandments.[7] More pertinently, in this context, is that the Israelites wandered in the *wilderness* for forty years. I suggest a key text in understanding the temptation of Jesus is Deut 8:2, where we read:

---

4. See Matt 13:24–30, 36–43. See also Matt 25:41 for his depiction of the ultimate destruction of the devil and his demons.

5. This personification of evil came back with the Jews from the Babylonian exile and influenced Second Temple literature (and the New Testament). Prior to that, *God* was seen as the source of good and evil in the Old Testament; see, for example, Isa 30:19–20; 45:5–7; Lam 3:37–38; Job 1:21; 2:10; 42:11; Amos 3:5–6. Modern sensibilities can belittle the power of evil and its reality.

6. Matt 4:2; Luke 4:2.

7. Exod 34:27–28. See also 1 Kgs 19:7–12, where Elijah had a similar fast, ending with a powerful encounter with God. Compare 1 Kgs 19:5, 7 with Matt 4:11.

The Jesus I Didn't Know I Didn't Know

> Remember the long way that the LORD your God has led you these forty years in the wilderness, in order to humble you, *testing you to know what was in your heart*, whether or not you would keep his commandments.[8]

The overall picture then is that God—through Moses—rescued the chosen people from bondage in Egypt through the waters of the Red Sea to ultimately take them into the Promised Land. In an analogous way, Matthew sees Jesus as passing through the waters of baptism to ultimately save God's people from the slavery of sin and bring them into the kingdom of God.[9] This testing of Jesus in the wilderness for forty days and nights therefore parallels the testing of Israel in the wilderness for forty years. Regrettably, the people of Israel failed that test; they did not trust God to provide for their basic needs[10] and they also worshiped idols.[11] The issue at stake here is, "Will Jesus pass the test?"[12]

The devil's first temptation to a vulnerable Jesus acknowledges his basic need of food after a long fast. The devil says: "If you are the Son of God, command these stones to become loaves of bread."[13] First, it's unlikely that the devil is doubting Jesus is God's Chosen One by stressing the word *if* in that verse. Later, in Matthew's description of an exorcism, even the demon addresses Jesus as the Son of God.[14] (Be patient, we will consider the meaning of Son of God in the next chapter! For the moment, consider the title to be synonymous with Messiah.) I suggest a better translation is *"Since you are the Son of God, command these stones to become loaves of bread."* So, the temptation is not to cause Jesus to doubt his true

---

8. Italics added.

9. See Matt 1:21; 20:28. Matthew uses the term "kingdom of heaven"; I use Luke's term to avoid confusion. This will be discussed further in chapter 6.

10. See Exod 16:1—17:7. This contains the account of God's provision of manna and quail, plus the water from the rock incident.

11. Recall the famed golden calf. See Exod 32.

12. Note that in, for example, Exod 4:22-23 and Hos 11:1, Israel is referred to as God's son. In the same vein, Jesus becomes a representation of the new Israel and is to be tested in a similar way as the original people in the wilderness.

13. Matt 4:3.

14. See Matt 8:29. See also Matt 8:16; 12:22-37; 17:14-20.

The Temptation of Jesus

identity—although the devil would have welcomed that outcome too—but to discover the character of Jesus while under pressure and to ascertain *what kind of messiah he will be*.[15] Will he, for example, perform miracles for personal gain? (In this specific case, to provide food for himself.) Second, the connection to the experience of Israel in the wilderness becomes crystal clear when we read the very next verse in Deuteronomy 8:

> [The LORD your God] humbled you by letting you hunger, then by feeding you with manna, with which neither you nor your ancestors were acquainted, in order to make you understand that one does not live on bread alone, but by every word that comes from the mouth of the LORD.[16]

You will obviously recognize that the latter part was Jesus's reply to the devil.[17] Consequently, part of the test was simply, "Will the Messiah trust God to provide for his basic human needs?" The Israelites in the wilderness doubted and moaned, yet God did graciously supply them with manna, quail, and water.[18] As becomes clear later in the Gospel, the kind of messiah Jesus would become is one who would willingly experience human suffering, trusting that God's provision would come at the appropriate time.

In the second temptation, the devil mystically takes Jesus to the roof of the temple in Jerusalem[19] and says:

> Since/if you are the Son of God, throw yourself down;
> for it is written, "He will command his angels concerning

---

15. Matthew has already explicitly told his readers of Jesus's identity as Messiah. See Matt 1:1, 17–18; 2:4.

16. Deut 8:3.

17. Matt 4:4. It is not insignificant to a Jewish audience that Jesus is quoting from the Torah, which is attributed to Moses.

18. Exod 16:1—17:7. This connection is present in Jesus feeding the multitudes in Matt 14:13–21 and more explicitly in John 6.

19. Matt 4:5. Referring to Jerusalem as the holy city has eschatological overtones. See Matt 27:53; Rev 11:2; 21:2, 10.

The Jesus I Didn't Know I Didn't Know

you," and "On their hand they will bear you up, so that you will not dash your foot against a stone."[20]

Again I suggest the underlying question is, "What kind of messiah will Jesus be?" Will he start a new movement with a spectacular, miraculous entrance that will compel people to believe in him? What the devil is asking is not obviously sinful, as such, and he cleverly—even cunningly—backs it up with a supportive prooftext from Scripture.[21] Jesus answers the devil, "It is also written: 'Do not put the Lord your God to the test,'"[22] which is an appropriate rebuttal. Moreover, we cannot overlook the fact that this quote from Deut 6 continues with an encouraging word to endure:

> Do what is right and good in the sight of the LORD, so that it may go well with you, and so that you may go in and occupy the good land that the LORD swore to your ancestors to give you, thrusting out all your enemies from before you, as the LORD promised.[23]

(Incidentally, according to Matthew, the last time Jesus would hear the phrase, "Since/if you are the Son of God" was when he was being mocked on the cross by the crowds.[24])

In the third temptation, the devil takes Jesus to a very high mountain and shows him all the kingdoms of the world and their splendor. "All this I will give you," he said, "if you will fall down and worship me."[25] This is the temptation to seek prestige and power—to rule the world, a role played at the time by the Roman emperor. It also pertains to worshiping idols, a test Israel failed in the wilderness.[26] The tension between the kingdom of God and the kingdoms of this world, represented by the Jewish and Roman authorities,

---

20. Matt 4:6, citing Ps 91:11, 12.

21. This perhaps highlights how well-intentioned interpretations of the Bible can become a vehicle for evil.

22. Matt 4:7 NIV, citing Deut 6:16.

23. Deut 6:18–19.

24. See Matt 27:39–44.

25. Matt 4:8–9 NIV. Recall that "being like God" is a feature of the temptation in the garden of Eden (Gen 3:5).

26. See Deut 6:4–19; Exod 32.

The Temptation of Jesus

runs throughout the Gospel.[27] Later on, Matthew relates how the mother of James and John wants her two sons to sit at Christ's right and left when his kingdom arrives.[28] And Jesus responds, "Whoever wishes to be great among you must be your servant, . . . just as the Son of Man came not to be served but to serve, and to give his life [as] a ransom for many."[29] This, then, is the kind of messiah that Jesus would become. In the end, Jesus rebukes the devil in good Jewish fashion, citing a passage connected with the *Shema*, which Jews pray daily:

> Hear, O Israel: The LORD is our God, the LORD alone (or the LORD is one). You shall love the LORD your God with all your heart, and with all your soul, and with all your might. . . .[30] Worship the LORD your God, and serve only him.[31]

Since Jesus resists three temptations—always a noteworthy number signifying special emphasis in the Bible—he passes the test with his integrity intact, and so his ministry begins.

I have always found the story of the temptation of Jesus a little odd. If the incident is a genuinely historical moment, it was very private to Jesus because there were no human witnesses. That being the case, why did Jesus feel the need to relate the incident to his disciples? Only Matthew and Luke provide the details of the story, and their close similarity suggests a common source. However, the author of the book of Hebrews seems to have been aware of this tradition, for he writes that in Jesus we do not have someone "who is unable to sympathize with our weaknesses, but we have one who in every respect has been tested as we are, yet without sin."[32] This statement is only meaningful if those temptations were

---

27. See Matt 12:22–30 for a discussion concerning the kingdoms of Satan and God.

28. See Matt 20:20–28.

29. Matt 20:26–28. The meaning of Son of Man will be discussed in the next chapter.

30. Deut. 6:4–5.

31. Matt 4:10 (adapting Deut. 6:13). See also Matt 22:36–38.

32. Heb 4:15. The NIV has "tempted" instead of "tested." See also Heb 2:14–18.

The Jesus I Didn't Know I Didn't Know

truly *real* for Jesus. In other words, he could have succumbed to at least one of them. The writer of Hebrews evidently thought that was the case—and so do I; Jesus was truly human.[33] This is why his determination to obey his understanding of God's will is mentioned frequently in the New Testament. For example, Paul stresses that we too can become God's adopted children because of the faithfulness of Jesus Christ.[34] Although I find those words from Hebrews to be encouraging, I suggest the account of the temptation of Jesus has a different purpose. It is not, as it is often portrayed, a how-to-overcome-temptation story. As emphasized earlier, it is a character-defining narrative that highlights what kind of messiah Jesus would be, a purpose that becomes clearer in light of the previously mentioned Old Testament texts.

There is a further aspect to the temptation of Jesus account to consider, namely one of authority. Just as Jesus's later verbal sparring with the Jewish religious leaders is to be understood as publicly establishing—or demonstrating—his legitimate authority for ministry, the fact that Jesus gets the verbal upper hand over the devil also represents a victory. (Of course, this does not mean Jesus didn't encounter temptation—or the devil—again.[35]) More specifically, through this exchange, Jesus gains sufficient authority over Satan to be able to exorcize demons. While this may seem bizarre to us, the temptation account provides an explanation to the reader as to how Jesus also became an exorcist. In fact, Jesus is later accused by his critics of being in league with the devil; how else could he be able to control demons? Jesus laughs off his opposition, saying, "No one can enter a strong man's house without first tying him up."[36] In other

---

33. Not least because of Christianity's later doctrine of the Trinity, I believe Jesus was also fully divine. Some are troubled by Christ's divinity because they then think it would be *impossible* for Jesus to sin, which—of course—renders the temptation story meaningless. Not only does this approach ignore or deny Jesus's humanity, it negates the basis of the whole temptation/testing account. I suggest this line of thinking is unwise and unhelpful—and misses the key point of the narrative, as explained above.

34. See, for example, the NET translations of Gal 2:16, 20; Rom 3:22; Eph 3:12; Phil 3:9.

35. See Mark 14:32–42; Matt 16:23; 26:36–46, 53; Luke 4:13; 22:39–46.

36. See Mark 3:27 NIV; Matt 12:29.

words, he denies his opponent's logic. Jesus is not partnering with the devil; instead, he has *restrained* him. The temptation narrative is then, in part, a story of how Jesus established his authority over Satan. And that's one of those things I didn't know I didn't know.

Chapter 4

The Titles of Jesus

As I have already said, Mark tells his readers in the very first verse that Jesus is the Messiah, the Son of God. In addition to the title Messiah, Matthew adds Son of David and Son of Abraham.[1] These descriptions already meant something to their readers, whereas to us they need explaining. The opening chapter of John's Gospel has a long catalogue of titles and descriptions. He begins by claiming Jesus is the Word made flesh[2] and goes on to say Jesus is:

> the light of all people,[3]
> the Son of God,[4]
> the Messiah or God's Anointed One (in Hebrew)
> or the Christ (in Greek),[5]
> the Lamb of God,[6]
> rabbi or teacher,[7]
> Jesus of Nazareth,[8]

1. Mark 1:1 NIV; Matt 1:1.
2. John 1:14, 1.
3. John 1:4–5, 7–9.
4. John 1:18, 34, 49.
5. John 1:17, 41.
6. John 1:29, 36. This refers to Jesus as the (new) Passover lamb, a key theme in John's Gospel.
7. John 1:38, 49.
8. John 1:45 NIV. Jesus is also described as "the one Moses wrote about" and "of whom the prophets also wrote."

The Titles of Jesus

the son of Joseph,[9]
the King of Israel,[10]
and the Son of Man.[11]

What a list! Some of those titles stress the humanness of Jesus, others say that Jesus has the closest possible relationship with God[12] and is even the co-creator of all that is.[13] Are these claims wrong or misguided? I suggest we need to reserve judgment and read on. The author presents some of these titles through the words of witnesses like John the Baptist, Andrew, Philip, and Nathanael. They are using such expressions to describe the roles and functions of the person and work of Jesus. Yes, we can be confused and overwhelmed by all these descriptive titles, but John's readers were no doubt aware of at least some of those names. Moreover, as John is laying out all these titles, he is not saying we can pick and choose from them as we like. No, they are *all* applicable to Jesus, and as the Gospel continues, the meaning of all these names will be expanded, transformed, or redefined by the words of other witnesses, by those of Jesus himself, and by his actions—including his death and resurrection. Up until now I have not tried to explain the meaning of titles like Messiah, Son of God, Son of Man, etc. Let's briefly consider some of the key titles in this short chapter.

MESSIAH

It is often joked that people think Christ is Jesus's last name! It is not. It is a title: Jesus the Christ. But what does Christ mean? It is the Greek equivalent of the Hebrew messiah, which also means the anointed (or chosen) one. Sometimes I wonder if the name Jesus

---

9. John 1:45. John has already revealed to his readers what he considers Jesus's true origins to be in his prologue (John 1:1–14). Consequently, through the eyes of faith we know that Joseph is not Jesus's natural father. This introduces a tension that John will revisit later. See John 6:42; 7:40–42.
10. John 1:49.
11. John 1:51.
12. John 1:18.
13. John 1:3.

The Jesus I Didn't Know I Didn't Know

Christ has, over time, inadvertently made Jesus "white," whereas Jesus the Messiah reminds us of his Jewish identity. Indeed, all the New Testament titles need to be seen in a Jewish context, although, as we will see, some of them have related resonances for non-Jewish audiences too.

Within Jewish tradition, priests, prophets, and kings were anointed as part of their inauguration.[14] Being anointed therefore implies being chosen by God for a specific purpose or task. In first-century Judaism, however, messiah was widely understood as God's anointed king, primarily as a political and military savior who would defeat Israel's oppressors and establish God's kingdom or reign.[15] Consequently, to claim Jesus as Messiah is to state that God is acting distinctively and decisively in Jesus. Put another way, Jesus is the agent through whom God is working in an unprecedented and unrepeatable way.

With respect to the above cultural expectation, clearly Jesus did not bring about the liberation the Jewish people had anticipated. Yet the writers of the Synoptic Gospels—Matthew, Mark, and Luke—still make this twofold claim:

1. God personally anointed Jesus at his baptism (and affirmed it at the transfiguration[16]) and, consequently, Jesus is deemed to have a divine mandate.
2. Jesus is more than a prophet. He is the Messiah, which is also associated with the kingly titles Son of David and King of Israel/of the Jews.

That being the case, this implies that these authors—and John too—understood Jesus to be redefining what messiah means through his teaching and actions—and that he was divinely authorized to do so.

---

14. For example, Exod 28:41; Lev 21:10; 1 Kgs 19:16; Isa 61:1; Ps 18:50; 105:15; 1 Sam 15:1; 2 Sam 2:4. The understanding of Christ as "prophet, priest, and king" came much later in Christian theology.

15. This is evident in the conversation between King Herod and the Magi, where king of the Jews and messiah seem to be used interchangeably. See Matt 2:2–4.

16. See Matt 17:1–8; Mark 9:2–8; Luke 9:28–36. The transfiguration will be discussed in chapter 7.

The Titles of Jesus

In that sense, Jesus was turning the Jewish worldview upside down. Moreover, because Jesus saw his kingdom message as extending to non-Jews too, this implies turning the whole world upside down as well. This viewpoint can be rejected, of course; after all, Jesus was killed! Nevertheless, the Gospel writers remain convinced that Jesus is the Messiah, and their respective Gospels explain why. Consequently, we cannot properly understand the Gospels without appreciating the more nuanced meanings of this distinctly Jewish title and its implications.

SON OF GOD

The title Son of God has both Jewish and Greco-Roman connotations. This term should not be seen in a trinitarian sense here—in other words, that Jesus is divine. This understanding was developed over the next few centuries. Rather, Son of God was a multifaceted title that had subtle yet profound meanings to both Jews and non-Jews alike. For Jews, Son of God was used in association with an adopted royal son upon his coronation,[17] a name for angelic beings,[18] a particularly wise or righteous individual,[19] or someone highly honored by God. For non-Jews, the term was linked to a divine being, such as a nonhuman (e.g., a demigod) capable of superhuman feats or a recently deceased Caesar who was subsequently viewed as a divine personage. The specialness of the individual is implied in both cultural contexts, and consequently a Son of God belongs to God. This aspect of being chosen by God means that in

---

17. See Ps 2:7.
18. See Gen 6:2; Job 1:6 NET.
19. Wis 2:12–20; Sir 4:10. The Wisdom of Solomon is among the deuterocanonical books, along with Sirach, Baruch, Maccabees, and a few other works. These scrolls were written in Greek, not Hebrew (although some Hebrew fragments have been found) and—at some point—were included in the LXX Greek translation of the Hebrew Scriptures. Regardless of their formal status as Scripture, these books were known and read in the first century, and there are allusions to these books in the New Testament. They therefore provide important insight into the Jewish mindset of the day.

The Jesus I Didn't Know I Didn't Know

the first-century Judeo-Christian context, Son of God (or just Son) was virtually synonymous with Messiah.[20]

SON OF MAN

Unlike Son of God, Son of Man would have been an unfamiliar term to non-Jews, as it is for us today. On one level, Son of Man signifies belonging to man and is the equivalent of human being or mortal—an expression frequently used in, for example, Ezekiel.[21] In New Testament times, however, Son of Man also alluded to a popular apocalyptic vision from the book of Daniel.[22] It was thought that God was reserving in heaven an actual transcendent being—the Son of Man—who would come from heaven at the end of history and inaugurate the kingdom of God. According to the vision, all nations and peoples of every language would worship him, and his reign would never end.[23] Curiously, the Gospel writers (and the disciples) do not use this title themselves for Jesus; rather, Jesus uses it to—somewhat obliquely—reference himself.[24] This, then, is a somewhat mysterious and, perhaps at times, ambiguous or confusing title.[25] Nevertheless, given that the first-century understanding of Son of Man was not merely that of a mortal being but of someone

---

20. For example, see John 11:27; 20:31.

21. For example, see Ezek 2:1–10 NIV. Son of Man is used ninety-three times in Ezekiel to refer to the prophet!

22. See Dan 7:13–14. In Matt 13:40–43 not only is there a reference to the Son of Man, but he cites Dan 3:6 and alludes to Dan 12:3. Such literary connections are evidence that the book of Daniel was well-known to Matthew's readers. The Son of Man is also mentioned in 2 Esdras/4 Ezra and in the parables/similitudes of Enoch as a preexistent, messianic figure.

23. This vision speaks of all nations worshiping the Son of Man, not just Jews. There are many Old Testament prophetic oracles that essentially say the same thing, or proclaim that all people are invited to the messianic banquet, e.g., Isa 25:6.

24. The Gospel writers use this expression in various nuanced ways, such as an equivalent of Messiah, or with reference to both Jesus's ministry and sufferings, or to Jesus as eschatological judge.

25. See, for example, John 12:34.

The Titles of Jesus

transcendent—or from God—this has incarnational overtones. In which case Son of Man is, ironically, a theocentric title!

What I didn't know I didn't know was this counterintuitive meaning of the Son of Man and its connection with the title Son of God. For many Christians, the name Son of God is assumed to be pointing to the divinity of Jesus because of a prior belief in the Trinity. But as I have just indicated, this is not how first-century readers would have understood the term. However, that bias leads us to a further (erroneous) assumption, namely that Jesus wouldn't have wanted to draw attention to himself with such a title as it would have been blatantly blasphemous to Jews, and it could therefore have jeopardized his ministry.[26] Consequently, so I thought, Jesus preferred the title Son of Man to downplay his divinity and emphasize his humanity. After all, Son of God implies belonging to God, whereas Son of Man—on the face of it—denotes belonging to humankind. However, given that Son of Man—through the lens of Daniel's vision—points to a mysterious Jewish figure from God, these assumptions are mistaken and misleading. For Jesus to use Son of Man to refer to himself is an explosive title to the discerning Jew.[27] It is not the opposite of the Son of God, as I had assumed, but actually points to the divine, for the Son of Man is God's agent in history.

LORD

The Greek word for lord (*kyrios*) is used as (a) a title of respect, like sir in English, and (b) a synonym for master, as in someone with authority over others, such as a slave owner. However, the widely read Greek LXX translation of the Hebrew Scriptures (the texts Christians call the Old Testament) uses *kyrios* for God's personal name, YHWH, and is written as LORD in the Bible. The same Greek word was also commonly used for the Roman emperor. Consequently,

---

26. Regardless of the (mistaken) divinity element, Herod, for example, would still be concerned to hear of someone openly claiming to be the messiah or the son of God because of those titles' political connotations.

27. For example, consider the reaction at Jesus's trial with the Jewish religious authorities: Mark 14:62–64; Matt 26:64–66.

The Jesus I Didn't Know I Didn't Know

using this term with reference to Jesus raises the issue of patriotism for Romans and blasphemy for Jews. The specific meaning of lord can sometimes be resolved from its contextual usage; at other times it is ambiguous. Perhaps this is deliberate by the Gospel writers. After all, they confess the post-resurrection Jesus as Lord not as an honorific title but as someone worthy of prime loyalty and adoration. That last point is important. Various New Testament writers make it clear that Jesus is actually worthy of *worship*—which is blasphemous for Jews, for God alone is praiseworthy.[28] This practice came about because of the early church's belief in the resurrection and in the implications of that event for the identity of Jesus in relation to God the Father. This Christian perspective cannot be overlooked, and it ties in with the complex meaning of Jesus as Lord.[29]

THE WORD MADE FLESH

John's Gospel starts with some of the most powerful and evocative phrases concerning Jesus in the whole of the New Testament:

> In the beginning was the Word, and the Word was with God, and the Word was God. He was in the beginning with God. All things came into being through him, and without him not one thing came into being. What has come into being in him was life, and the life was the light of all people. The light shines in the darkness, and the darkness did not overcome it.... And the Word became flesh and lived among us, and we have seen his glory, the glory as of a father's only son, full of grace and truth.[30]

The author does not begin with a birth narrative but with words (or perhaps a hymn) that point to a cosmic, preexistent Word (Greek: *logos*) and that Word's relationship to the world. Even the opening

---

28. See Matt 14:33; 28:9, 17; John 9:38. Note that the word "worship" is also mentioned *three* times in the visit of the Magi (Matt 2:2, 8, 11 NIV).

29. Paul mentions "Jesus is Lord" in 1 Cor 12:3 in the context of an authentic Spirit-inspired confessional statement.

30. John 1:1–5, 14. See also John 8:58 for another preexistence reference.

The Titles of Jesus

phrase "in the beginning" reminds the reader of Gen 1:1.[31] There we read that the divine spirit was moving over the primordial waters and that God *spoke* and creation came to be.[32] Words are accompanied by deeds. When God speaks, things happen! God also spoke through the prophets. Later in Jewish thinking, wisdom is personified and is also presented as being before the beginning of the world working alongside God.[33] To a Jew, then, God's word (or voice), wisdom, and spirit are the means through which God works in the world.

In the Greco-Roman world, the notion of the word had philosophical roots. The (divine) *logos* was understood to be the supreme rational principle that underlies all that is. It is the reason the universe continues to exist and maintains order rather than chaos.[34] Since reason and wisdom can be considered twins, or closely connected, John's non-Jewish audience would have appreciated the bold claims that he makes in his introduction.

John's punchline is profound and stunning: *The Word became flesh and lived among us*—in the person of Jesus.[35] For John, then, Jesus is the embodiment of the preexistent, creative, divine Word, which enables him to assert that "all things came into being through him." This language adapts the Hebrew understanding of divine word and wisdom and enfleshes them in Jesus. Anyone interested in the Creator God and the crazy notion that such a God has entered history in human form—in a particular time and place—would be inquisitive enough to read more. Yes, some might be inclined to dismiss this assertion as ridiculous, but are we not just a little bit curious as to why a seemingly sane author would make such a daring statement?

---

31. Evidence that this is deliberate is found in John's repeated use of "the next day" (John 1:29, 35, 43).

32. See also Ps 33:6; 107:20; Isa 55:11; Jer 23:29.

33. See Prov 8:22–31. Note that this genre is poetry.

34. *Logos*, the Greek for "word," is the root of *-ology*, the ending of various academic disciplines.

35. See John 1:14.

Chapter 5

The Claims of Jesus

The Gospel writers tell us about the life of Jesus, including his teachings and miracles, based on a well-established oral tradition that was already in wide circulation.[1] They also present various sayings that Jesus reportedly said about himself. The statements are succinct and memorable, and for that reason I have no grounds to doubt Jesus actually said them. If Matthew and Luke repeat Mark's statements verbatim, that strongly supports the historicity of those words (and actions) of Jesus. Of course, just because people say something about themselves doesn't automatically mean it is true! However, the Gospel writers' inclusion of this material affirms that they—and the communities they represent—believed them to be authentic, accurate, and factual. And we, like later readers of the Gospels, are left wondering what all this means.

We will simply consider two claims of Jesus in this chapter, one from the Synoptic Gospels (Matthew, Mark, and Luke) and one from John's account. What I didn't know I didn't know was the necessity of seeing these claims in the context of the Old Testament, something Jesus's original audience and the Gospel readers would have readily appreciated. We cannot divorce the New Testament

---

1. The Gospel writers may well have had access to other written documents in circulation that are now lost, such as the proposed Q source of Jesus's sayings for Matthew and Luke. But even they almost certainly originated from an oral tradition. Also remember these documents were written in Greek, and Jesus's mother tongue was Aramaic.

The Claims of Jesus

from the Old—as some have tried to do. As we saw in the birth narrative in chapter 1, Matthew was at pains to show the continuity of his account with Israel's long history. Only with these links intact will we be able to understand the extraordinary and audacious claims of Jesus.

"THE SON OF MAN IS LORD OF THE SABBATH"

Sabbath observance would have been a key issue for the original readers of the Gospels, whether they were Jewish or non-Jewish Christians. Religious practice in multi-ethnic Christianity was—and still can be—a real source of division. And such activities were made more complicated by the early church's swift adoption of meeting on the first day of the week, Sunday—the day of resurrection. "Keeping the Sabbath holy" was—and is—very important to Jews; after all, it is one of the Ten Commandments.[2] It was a sign that they belonged to the true God, the Creator of the world, who also rested—or so we are told—on the seventh day.[3] It was, in a sense, a weekly reminder of the need for *shalom*: peace with God, with each other, and with creation. Keep in mind that the details of what one was required to do in order to keep the Sabbath holy were not clearly specified in the Mosaic law, and so different rabbis might disagree over precisely what is a violation of the law.

The Pharisees, however, had a reputation of being nitpicking rulekeepers. This group of laypeople often gets a bad rap in the Gospels, and this has tragically—and regrettably—added further fuel to the fires of anti-Semitism. We need to see the Pharisees' actions in the context of the religious nationalism of the day. Their zeal for the Jewish people to keep the law of Moses followed from their terrible experience of exile. They thought that the more the people followed the law, the more likely it was that God would dramatically step into history and vindicate Israel to the world in the way that they

---

2. Exod 20:8–11. There were three things that were imperative to devout Jews, namely, circumcision, dietary restrictions, and keeping the Sabbath.

3. Gen 2:2–3.

understood from the prophets. In their minds, if the Jewish people continually disobeyed God's commandments, God would, at the very least, postpone that ultimate day of rescue. That's why they stressed purity and close observance of the law.[4]

With that background information, consider the following story relayed early in Mark's Gospel.[5] As the disciples went through a farmer's field on the Sabbath, they picked some of the heads of wheat on their way—and were spotted doing so by keen Pharisees. This act was not regarded as theft, since they were not using a sickle,[6] but they were deemed to be technically breaking the law as they were "reaping" a crop on the Sabbath. When the Pharisees spoke to Jesus, they obviously expected him to stop his disciples' cavalier behaviour at once. But he did not rebuke them; instead he provocatively appealed to an obscure precedent pertaining to King David. David effectively committed sacrilege by taking holy bread from the high priest for himself and his armed followers, since they were in dire need of food.[7] Now it was well understood that Sabbath laws could be set aside in an emergency. But Jesus and his disciples were not starving, so why allude to King David's situation? Mark does not explicitly answer that question, but Jesus then continues with the well-known line: "The Sabbath was made for people, not

---

4. As a group, the Pharisees had been in existence for about two hundred years and were entirely self-chosen. They had no authority to make laws or enforce them, but they did have considerable influence on ordinary people who respected their expertise on Israel's ancient laws and living traditions. Some of the Pharisees were—no doubt—wise, devout, honorable men. Given their general stress on piety and living holy lives, others of the Pharisees seem to have set themselves up as guardians of the morality of the people in the public eye.

5. Mark 2:23—3:6; see also Matt 12:1–14 and Luke 6:1–11 for essentially the same account.

6. Deut 23:25.

7. See 1 Sam 21:1–6. Mark makes an error: it was Ahimelech—not Abiathar—who was high priest at the time. (Matthew and Luke omit the mention of Abiathar.) Moreover, there were more recent situations when the Sabbath-keeping principle was laid aside in an emergency, for example, see 1 Macc 2:34–41 (and chapter 4, page 31, footnote 19).

The Claims of Jesus

people for the Sabbath. For this reason, the Son of Man is Lord *even* of the Sabbath."[8]

Earlier in the Gospel, Mark had established that Jesus speaks and acts with astonishing authority.[9] In the political and religious context of the day, an understandable question in the minds of the Jewish leaders was: "To what end will Jesus exercise his authority?" And Mark has already told his readers that Jesus said, "The Son of Man has authority on earth *to forgive sins.*"[10] This, in the Pharisees' minds, was blasphemy.[11] And now we have another Son of Man statement, that Jesus is master even of the Sabbath—of the Mosaic law itself! These further forthright claims flesh out what Christ's authority means. This repeated identification with the visionary Son of Man signifies that the kingdom of God has arrived; God's prophesied reign is breaking in. God is doing something new, and Christ's forgiveness and healings are signs of that greater reality. So, to what end will Christ use his self-evident authority? The answer is to totally change our understanding of the world as we know it. Even Israel's God-given laws would need to be seen in a new light because the Messiah had come. It is he, Jesus, who has the authority to interpret the law.[12]

This is affirmed in the next Sabbath incident at the synagogue. We can imagine the scene: the Pharisees are on the front row, in the place of honor, watching and waiting to see what Jesus will do next.[13] We are told there was a man with a withered hand present.[14] The Greek word implies that the man was not born with that illness, but that his arm was effectively paralyzed for some reason,

---

8. Mark 2:27-28 NET (italics added). See also Matt 12:5-7 for his added explanatory preamble.

9. Mark 1:21-28.

10. Mark 2:10 (italics added).

11. Mark 2:7. It also challenged the authority of the temple system itself—and the power of the religious elite.

12. This is explicit in the Sermon on the Mount, where Jesus repeatedly says, "You have heard it said, *but I say*" (see Matt 5:21-48).

13. See Matt 23:2, 6; Luke 14:7.

14. Mark 3:1; see also Matt 12:9-14; Luke 6:6-11. Luke adds that it was the man's right hand.

The Jesus I Didn't Know I Didn't Know

and therefore he could not work.[15] The Pharisees knew that Jesus could perform miracles; there was no doubt about that in their minds—as some people have today. The key question was a matter of religious law: would he heal on the Sabbath? So Jesus challenges them, "Is it lawful to do good or do harm on the Sabbath, to save life or to kill?"[16] This would not have been disputed by any rabbi. Doing merciful and necessary acts that save lives always took precedence over Sabbath obligations in an emergency. Consequently, a woman in childbirth could be helped on the Sabbath. More generally, though, infections and injuries could be kept from getting worse, but they could not be actively made better. The man's withered hand was obviously a nonurgent case. Jesus could simply wait until sundown—when the Sabbath ended—and heal the man then. Jesus demonstrates what being Lord of the Sabbath means and thereby takes the initiative and forces the issue. Jesus tells the man to raise his hand, not to embarrass him, but to expose the others for their lack of sympathy towards him. Jesus was both angered and grieved by their hardness of heart.[17]

And the man's hand is simply healed. It is not clear what Jesus actually *does* in terms of the healing. All he *says* (to the man) is, "Stretch out your hand."[18] Nevertheless, the outcome is attributed to Christ's presence. What is lost in all this drama is that nothing Jesus physically does could be construed as working on the Sabbath. Theologically, however, the man's condition signifies death, and his healing, life. Jesus cannot, however, heal a stubborn heart. And whatever "keeping the Sabbath holy" may mean in practice, it is not to be in a spirit of hardheartedness. When we forget to love,

---

15. In the fragments of the *Gospel of the Nazarenes*, and with reference to Matt 12:10–13, the man is described as a stonemason. He asks Jesus to restore his health so that he need not beg for his food.

16. Mark 3:4.

17. Mark 3:5. It is not unlike that today: well-meaning Christians often create a specific litmus test that is supposedly meant to examine the genuineness of someone's faith or belief system and, in the process, miss the whole point of the gospel.

18. Mark 3:5; Matt 12:13; Luke 6:10. And we are then simply told, "He stretched it out, and his hand was restored."

The Claims of Jesus

forgive, and serve, and replace these with legalism, then the life-giving intent of the Sabbath has been lost.

The Pharisees' response is not amazement, as their reaction had been earlier, but cold hostility.[19] By consciously invoking a controversy with the religious authorities, Jesus puts himself at risk. Since Mark places this incident early in his Gospel, it seems that this argument about the Sabbath played a critical role in the life of Jesus and was one of the factors that eventually led to his death. At least that is how Mark, with the benefit of hindsight, portrays it. We are told, "The Pharisees went out immediately and began plotting with the Herodians, as to how they could assassinate him."[20] Ironically, their determination to see him die was certainly against the law.

Let's not focus on the important practical, ethical, and social issues themselves without first zooming back to see the bigger picture. Even at this early stage of Christ's ministry, those religious leaders correctly perceived that Jesus was offering a radical vision of life with God. Jesus, however, did not scrap the concept of Sabbath. He was—and is—proclaiming, in word and deed, a new way of understanding who God is, and this is challenging for every generation. God is not confined to our religious rules, or to our perceptions of God, or to our assumptions concerning God's ways of working in the world. Moreover, because Jewish understanding of the Sabbath impacted not just their identity but wider social practices, Jesus was reconfiguring our relationship to God, not just as individuals but in the very structures of society as well. Such ethical and social reforms are very threatening and are resisted. The difficult truth is

---

19. Compare Mark 2:12 with 3:6.

20. Mark 3:6 NET; Matthew and Luke concur. Incidentally, the Herodians were not a well-defined political party but were likely wealthy aristocrats who were friends and retainers of Herod Antipas. The Herodians were continually coming into contact with the Romans and, consequently, some Pharisees would have considered them ritually unclean. Moreover, they are thought to have been willing to compromise and collaborate with the Roman authorities out of political expediency and self-interest. For Pharisees to be collaborating with the Herodians was therefore a sign of desperation. It was as if Jewish conservatives and the liberal wealthy elite were joining forces to entrap someone who might have upset the status quo. See also Mark 12:13; Matt 22:15–16.

The Jesus I Didn't Know I Didn't Know

that we would rather kill Jesus than be transformed by his message. In a similar way, when God gets too close to us—challenging us as Jesus confronted the religious order of his day—then we begin to construct ways and means to kill off God, too. In other words, we try to make God irrelevant. And when we make the rules, we become Lord of the Sabbath!

In the Synoptic Gospels, as we have just seen, when the religious leaders question Jesus's activities on the Sabbath, he uses it as an opportunity to explain the meaning of the Sabbath. In John's Gospel, however, Jesus uses the opportunity to reveal something about his identity.[21] John tells us that Jesus told his opponents, "My Father is always at his work to this very day, and I too am working."[22] What does this mean? After all, in Genesis we are told God rested on the Sabbath.[23] Is Jesus contradicting the supposed words of Moses? Not really. Jewish thinkers had come to understand that God *cannot* rest on the Sabbath, because creation continues: children are born, so new life is being given; people die, so their lives need to be judged. The work of God never stops. And Jesus says that, like his Father, he too is working to bring about "new life"—or healing in this case—even on the Sabbath.[24] The Jewish leaders don't dispute that aspect of Jesus's reply, but they are now even more upset because they understand him to be making himself *equal* with God—by calling God his own Father.[25] Words matter here; for *a* to equal *b*, they must both be independent of one another. The religious leaders are therefore confused. Jesus is not setting himself up as an alternative to God or as usurping God's authority. And so he goes on to carefully explain what he means without ever using the word equal.[26]

Jesus is not claiming equality with God, but *unity* with God, and he articulates this unity in terms of a father-son relationship.

21. See John 5:1-23; again, the context is one of healing on the Sabbath.
22. John 5:17 NIV.
23. Gen 2:2-3; Exod 20:11.
24. The healing can therefore be considered a sign of the new creation.
25. John 5:18. Their stated desire to kill him was for the ultimate, unforgivable sin of blasphemy—whose penalty was death by stoning. See Lev 24:16.
26. John 5:19-23.

The Claims of Jesus

Parents often teach their children lessons through their words and actions, and they are certainly not strangers to having their children imitate them. Children often repeat what they hear and copy gestures. (I sometimes find it scary when I catch myself unconsciously exhibiting my own dad's mannerisms!) Jesus says, "I tell you the solemn truth, the Son can do nothing on his own initiative, but only what he sees the Father doing."[27] This tells us Jesus is not independent of God. Instead, Jesus perfectly follows through with the Father's instructions. And because the Son's actions are exactly like those of the Father's, the Son is the clearest reflection of God the Father. According to John, then, Jesus understands his own identity as that of one who lives with unqualified devotion and obedience to the Father's will. Jesus is therefore like a faithful son who is fully apprenticed in his father's craft. They are unified in purpose and love. And because Jesus is utterly dependent upon the Father, Jesus is entrusted with the fullness of the Father's authority both to *give life*[28] and *to judge*,[29] two tasks that Jewish tradition agrees God does even on the Sabbath. Consequently, the works of Jesus in healing and in judgment are the works of the Father. That's why Jesus concludes: "Anyone who does not honor the Son does not honor the Father who sent him."[30]

This Father-Son relationship is a key theme in John's Gospel, yet even the disciples struggle to grasp what Jesus is saying. John later presents a major discourse of Jesus to his followers, just prior

---

27. John 5:19 NET, adding, "For whatever the Father does, the Son does likewise."

28. See John 5:20–21, 25–26. It is in this context that we are to understand John's later account of the raising of Lazarus. See John 11:1–44. It is there that John reports Jesus as saying, "I am the resurrection and the life" (John 11:25). Note that the Synoptic Gospels also give accounts of Jesus raising individuals from the dead. See Mark 5:21–24, 35–43; Luke 7:11–17, 8:49–56; Matt 9:18–26. Such mighty acts are linked to special, holy people. See also 1 Kgs 17:17–24; 2 Kgs 4:18–37; Acts 9:36–42, 20:7–12.

29. See John 5:27–30. The notion of Jesus as the divinely appointed (eschatological) judge is not unique to John. See, for example, Matt 7:21–23; 16:27; Acts 10:42; 17:31; 2 Cor 5:10; 2 Tim 4:1, 8.

30. John 5:23.

The Jesus I Didn't Know I Didn't Know

to his death.[31] After *all* that the disciples have witnessed, Philip nevertheless says, "Lord, show us the Father, and we will be satisfied."[32] To see the glory of God is the longing of every devout person; Moses wanted the same experience.[33] Jesus simply says to him, "Have I been with you all this time, Philip, and you still do not know me? Whoever has seen me has seen the Father."[34] Jesus goes on and effectively repeats what he said earlier to those religious leaders:

> Do you not believe that I am in the Father and the Father is in me? The words that I say to you I do not speak on my own; but the Father who dwells in me does his works.[35]

The question left lingering is whether Philip and the other disciples will believe this, given all that they have witnessed . . .

While the Synoptic Gospels may not emphasize the Father-Son relationship to the extent that John does, it is still present. In Matthew's and Luke's Gospels we read these words of Jesus:

> All things have been handed over to me by my Father; and no one knows the Son except the Father, and no one knows the Father except the Son and anyone to whom the Son chooses to reveal him.[36]

It seems that Jesus had come to see himself as being like a window to the living God. It is the Son who had the gift of drawing back the curtain to reveal the truth about God to all who care to see.[37]

Some people find that notion a bit unsettling or too exclusive. But Matthew, uniquely among the Gospel writers, then presents

---

31. See John 14—17.
32. John 14:8.
33. See Exod 33:18–23.
34. John 14:9.
35. John 14:10. Jesus then adds, "Believe me that I am in the Father and the Father is in me; but if you do not, then believe me because of the works themselves." See also John 5:36–37; 7:16–17; 10:37–38; 12:48–50.
36. Matt 11:27; Luke 10:22. The phrase "all things" is powerful and noteworthy; it frequently occurs in the New Testament and will be discussed further in chapter 8. Note that it is generally considered that Matthew and Luke were written *before* John's Gospel.
37. See also John 1:51.

The Claims of Jesus

us with some of the most reassuring words of Jesus in the New Testament:

> Come to me, all you who are weary and burdened, and I will give you rest. Take my yoke on you and learn from me, because I am gentle and humble in heart, and you will find rest for your souls. For my yoke is easy to bear, and my load is not hard to carry.[38]

These comforting words resonate with phrases from Jeremiah and the wisdom writer, Sirach.[39] What then does "take my yoke on you and learn from me" mean? A yoke is, of course, the wooden crosspiece that is fastened over the necks of two cattle and attached to the plow that they are to pull. What is important is that the two animals be of similar build, else the yoke is ill-fitting and uncomfortable and so chafes their shoulders. Moreover, in this misbalanced scenario, one animal would do more work than the other, and it would also be difficult to plough a furrow in a straight line. Rabbis customarily spoke of the "yoke of Torah" or of being bound to the law of Moses. In the hands of the religious leaders of Jesus's day, that yoke had become legalistic, petty, and burdensome for many Jews; it was anything but easy.

It is in light of that experience that Jesus says, "Come to me, all you who are weary and burdened, and I will give you rest." That is a powerful message of relief and hope for all who are racked by guilt and a sense of obligation, or who are tired of the word should, or who see religion as an impossible set of artificial rules. Astonishingly, Jesus then says, "Take *my yoke* on you and learn from *me*." He is in effect saying that he himself replaces Torah; learn from Jesus himself! Yes, Jesus is claiming that kind of authority, and this is underlined in Matthew's next section on Jesus being Lord of the Sabbath, where—as we saw earlier—Jesus claims to be the divinely-authorized interpreter of the Mosaic law.[40] The "rest for the soul"

---

38. Matt 11:28–30 NET.

39. Jer 6:16; Sir 51:23–27 (see chapter 4, page 31, footnote 19); see also Exod 33:14.

40. Matt 12:1–14, esp. 6, 8.

The Jesus I Didn't Know I Didn't Know

he promises is forgiveness. Putting these thoughts together, Jesus is being portrayed as the true giver of Sabbath rest.

I find it interesting, to say the least, that this twinning of the yoke of Jesus and Lord of the Sabbath in Matthew is surrounded by references to the prophet Isaiah. John the Baptist is languishing in Herod's prison and seems to be having doubts about Jesus.[41] (Jesus is not behaving how John anticipates the messiah to act.) Jesus responds to John's followers by quoting the prophet Isaiah who, speaking of the messiah, proclaimed: "The Spirit of the Sovereign LORD is on me, because the LORD has anointed me to proclaim good news to the poor. He has sent me to bind up the brokenhearted."[42] Later, after Jesus speaks about being Lord of the Sabbath, Matthew again cites Isaiah, who gives another summary of the kind of messiah who is to come—one of gentleness and mercy. The LORD says through Isaiah:

> Here is my servant whom I have chosen, the one I love, in whom I take great delight; I will put my Spirit on him, and he will proclaim justice to the nations.... A bruised reed he will not break, and a smoldering wick he will not snuff out, until he has brought justice through to victory. In his name the nations will put their hope.[43]

Those opening words remind us of those authenticating divine words at Jesus's baptism, which—of course—John the Baptist witnessed. In the saying "a bruised reed he will not break," we recognize that the messiah comes to rescue and save, not to compound a person's troubles with more burdens. The mission of Jesus is to bring about God's restoration wherever it is needed by gently leading people into God's healing love. Perhaps surprisingly, Isaiah's oracle ends with "in his name the *non-Jews* will put their hope."[44] Hope has a name—his name is Jesus. It is not the

---

41. Matt 11:2–15.

42. Isa 61:1 NIV; see also Isa 35:5–6; Matt 11:4–6. Luke also defines Jesus's ministry by quoting the same text. See Luke 4:14–21.

43. Matt 12:18–21 NET/NIV adapted. He cites Isa 42:1–4 LXX, not the Hebrew Scriptures.

44. Matt 12:21 ("Gentiles" has been replaced by "non-Jews" here; italics

The Claims of Jesus

Torah, the Mosaic law, that is the source of our hope. It is Jesus the Messiah. As the writer of Hebrews concludes, there is someone greater than Moses here![45]

"I AM THE GOOD SHEPHERD"

The writer of the fourth Gospel makes numerous bold claims about Jesus. Perhaps the most stunning words he places on the lips of Jesus are a well-known series of "I am" statements. Not only do they point to the identity of Jesus using familiar metaphors from everyday life, but the use of "I am" has meaningful resonances for Jews. It links back to Moses and the burning bush incident where God revealed God's own personal name as YHWH: "I AM WHO I AM."[46] According to John, Jesus says:

> I am the bread of life,[47]
> I am the light of the world,[48]
> I am the good shepherd,[49]
> I am the resurrection and the life,[50]
> I am the way, the truth, and the life,[51]
> and I am the true vine.[52]

These are all authoritative and provocative statements, which together with other "I am" sayings in John's Gospel reflect how John understands the uniqueness of Jesus the Messiah and his intimate connection with God the Father. Chapters could be written about

---

added). See also Isa 42:4 LXX.

45. See Heb 3:1–6. This is also implied in the transfiguration story, in that divine words are spoken concerning Jesus in the presence of Moses and Elijah; see Matt 17:1–8; Mark 9:2–8, Luke 9:28–36. This will be discussed in chapter 7.

46. Exod 3:14.

47. John 6:35, 51; see also Isa 55:1–3.

48. John 8:12; 9:5; see also Isa 42:6–7.

49. John 10:11, 14.

50. John 11:25–26.

51. John 14:6.

52. John 15:1, 5; see also Ps 80:8–18; Isa 5:1–7; Jer 2:21; Ezek 19:10–14; Hos 10:1.

The Jesus I Didn't Know I Didn't Know

each statement! I will consider only one here: "I am the good shepherd."[53] If Jesus is the good shepherd, then we are invited to be the sheep that hear and follow his voice. Consequently, these "I am" statements do not simply reveal who Jesus is but who he is *in relation* to others.

The image of the good shepherd is one of the most comforting and reassuring metaphors for Jesus in John's Gospel. In John 10, Jesus twice says that he is the good shepherd who lays down his life for the sheep.[54] Many Christians immediately make a connection with Ps 23 because of its familiar opening line: "The LORD is my shepherd." I suggest, however, that John's audience would have gone to a different Old Testament passage, one from Ezekiel. And this is another one of those things I didn't know I didn't know.

Ezekiel was an eccentric and mysterious prophet. He lived in Babylon and is therefore referred to as the prophet of the exile. But let's begin even further back in Israel's history. The emerging nation of Israel, having crossed the River Jordan and having had some notable military victories, was nevertheless living among the region's Canaanites and was ruled by judges. The last of those ruling judges was Samuel. Eventually the people wanted to have a king and be like all the other nations around them. Samuel warned them that this was not a good idea and that they were rejecting God as their true King.[55] But the people insisted and—perhaps surprisingly—God graciously conceded to their request, and so Samuel anointed Saul. Things began well, but King Saul became a disappointment. Then along came Kings David and Solomon, the so-called Golden Age of Israel. As time went on, the subsequent kings increasingly failed to trust God and disobeyed God's commandments. Eventually the country was broken up into two kingdoms. The Northern Kingdom of Israel was later taken over by the Assyrian Empire. And after that, the Babylonian Empire conquered the Assyrians and even the Southern Kingdom of Judah.

---

53. The image of Jesus as shepherd is suggested in the parable of the lost sheep (Luke 15:1–7; Matt 18:12–14) and explicit in Matt 25:31–46, where the Son of Man is compared to a shepherd.

54. See John 10:11, 14–15.

55. See 1 Sam 8.

The Claims of Jesus

Both of these conquests resulted in exile for the Jews. As the Jews wrestled with their sense of abandonment by God, they realized that it was they themselves who had failed to keep their side of the covenant. It was in this time of desperation and seeking hope that the prophet Ezekiel spoke.

In chapter 34, Ezekiel speaks an oracle that begins "woe to the shepherds of Israel who only take care of yourselves,"[56] which is a message directed at Israel's leaders, in particular its former kings. Ezekiel's indictment proclaims that the selfish kings had not strengthened the weak, nor healed the sick, nor bound up the injured. They had not searched for the lost nor brought back the strays. Instead, they had ruled harshly and brutally.[57] It is what Ezekiel says next that is so shocking: God is not going to begin again with another king. God is done with kings! But God is not done with the divine mission to rescue the chosen people; God will keep God's side of the covenant, because God is a trustworthy promise keeper. Nevertheless, God is going to do something very different:

> For this is what the Sovereign LORD says: *I myself* will search for my sheep and look after them. As a shepherd looks after his scattered flock . . . so will I look after my sheep. I will rescue them from all the places where they were scattered.[58]

God repeats that God will personally be their shepherd and will search for the lost and bring back the strays. God goes on to say that God will also bind up the injured and strengthen the weak and will shepherd the flock with justice.[59] All the things that the kings should have done and didn't do, God will bring about. God, speaking through the prophet Ezekiel, then says,

> I will set up over them one shepherd, my servant David, and he shall feed them: he shall feed them and be their shepherd. And I, the LORD, will be their God, and my

---

56. Ezek 34:2 NIV.
57. See Ezek 34:4.
58. Ezek 34:11–12 NIV (italics added). See also Jer 23:1–3.
59. See Ezek 34:15–16.

The Jesus I Didn't Know I Didn't Know

servant David shall be prince among them; I, the LORD, have spoken.[60]

This princely servant David was widely understood to be the messiah.

Just as Ezekiel—through the oracle—condemns the kings who failed in their responsibilities and led the people astray, so John has a not-so-subtle critique of the Pharisees, to whom Jesus is speaking in John 9—10. Jesus then says, "I am the good shepherd."[61] This daringly points to Ezek 34:15, where God says: "I myself will be the shepherd of my sheep." That ancient prophecy is being fulfilled implies John. God is at work among us.[62] Therefore expect the messiah to search for the lost and bring back the strays, to bind up the injured and strengthen the weak, and to lead the flock with justice. And the Gospel writers all portray the ministry of Jesus to be just that.

Jesus goes on to say,

> I am the good shepherd; I know my own and my own know me. . . . I have other sheep that do not come from this sheepfold. I must bring them too, and they will listen to my voice, so that there will be one flock and one shepherd.[63]

The Pharisees and others in the audience may have been puzzled by that statement, but John's readers understood, because many were non-Jews who were now part of that extended flock. The original sheep were the people of Israel, and Jesus was calling them from amongst his Jewish contemporaries. But, as Israel's prophets and wise writers—like Ezekiel—had always hinted, the God of Israel was never only interested in Israel; God's covenant with Abraham

---

60. Ezek 34:23–24; see also Ezek 37:24–25.

61. John 10:11. Note that the Greek word for "good" (*kalos*) that John uses to qualify shepherd does *not* mean morally good—although Jesus was that—but means model or exemplary. Furthermore, the contrast is between the model shepherd, who is prepared to die to protect his sheep, and the hired hand who runs way at the first sign of trouble.

62. See also John 4:34; 17:3–5.

63. John 10:14, 16 NET.

The Claims of Jesus

was to be a blessing to the *whole* world.[64] The other sheep would be those from every nation under heaven whom God earnestly desires to save through Jesus. Consequently, Jesus the Messiah is the shepherd of the whole world—to all those who will listen and respond to his voice. Jesus says he is the good shepherd, and *he* knows who are his sheep. Sadly, there are too many Christians who consider themselves to be the gatekeepers of heaven, confidently pronouncing who will be there and who won't.[65]

Jesus was even prepared to "lay down his life for the sheep."[66] Moreover, John tells us that Jesus was confident that in giving his life he would receive it back again.[67] This confidence was based on the intimacy of the relationship he has with the Father, as I mentioned earlier. Not only does this point to the inseparability of death and resurrection in John, but stresses that Jesus was not a victim or a martyr against his will. John seems to suggest that Jesus was somehow controlling the circumstances of his own death![68] Strange as it may seem to us, Jesus, in laying down his life for the sheep, freely chooses that path as the ultimate expression of his obedience to—and trust in—God.[69] This perceived understanding of Jesus's own relationship with the Father and his seemingly perverse willingness to die seem crazy to us. It was outrageous to his audience too. John tells us, "Many of them were saying, 'He has a demon and is out of his mind. Why listen to him?'"[70] The way John cleverly

---

64. See Gen 12:2–3.

65. A few verses earlier, in John 10:9 NIV, Jesus says, "I am the gate; whoever enters through me will be saved."

66. See John 10:11, 15.

67. See John 10:17–18.

68. See John 12:23–36.

69. On that point, it is important to recognize that John does *not* mention the agony of Jesus in Gethsemane. See Mark 14:32–42; Matt 26:36–46; Luke 22:39–46. Nor does John relate Jesus's anguished cry on the cross, "My God, my God, why have you forsaken me." See Matt 27:46; Mark 15:34.

70. John 10:20. And in v. 21 we read: "Others were saying, 'These are not the words of one who has a demon. Can a demon open the eyes of the blind?'" See also Mark 3:20–30, esp. 21, 30.

The Jesus I Didn't Know I Didn't Know

presents his material forces his readers—including us—to consider and respond to that question.

Speaking of sheep, it is worth reminding ourselves of Peter's post-resurrection commission in John 21. There Jesus asks Peter three times, "Do you love me?"[71] This is usually seen as reversing Simon Peter's denial of Jesus three times on the night of his trial.[72] Jesus personally commissions Peter with these words: "Feed my lambs; take care of my sheep."[73] Jesus, the good shepherd, gives him a job to do. This echoes the words he said at an earlier post-resurrection appearance: "As the Father has sent me, so I send you."[74] That commission, empowered by the Spirit, is to partner with God the Father and the risen Son in fulfilling the earlier prophecy from Ezekiel, where God says: "I will search for the lost and bring back the strays. I will bind up the injured and strengthen the weak.... I will shepherd the flock with justice."[75]

And talk of justice naturally leads us to politics . . .

---

71. See John 21:15–17.
72. See John 18:15–18, 25–27.
73. See John 21:15–17 NIV.
74. John 20:21.
75. Ezek 34:16 NIV.

Chapter 6

The Politics of Jesus

In choosing twelve disciples Jesus was more provocative and political than we sometimes think. That is because we often pigeonhole Jesus as being purely a *spiritual* man. However, there were twelve tribes of Israel, and so Jesus having twelve disciples would, to the discerning, be seen as him seeking to lead a new Israel from the River Jordan, where Jesus was baptized, into the Promised Land—otherwise known in the Gospels as the kingdom of God. While this notion might seem fanciful to some readers, Matthew makes many parallels between Jesus and Moses in his Gospel.[1]

In first-century Palestine, religious and political power were closely intertwined—as we will see in a moment. Moreover, just like John the Baptist, Jesus was often considered to be a prophet, and such people courageously spoke truth to power. Prophets were expected to call for religious purity and reform; that's just what prophets did. And Jesus was no exception. Consider, for example, the incident where Jesus overturns the tables of the money changers in the temple forecourt. Jesus saw this practice not just as corrupt profiteering, but as creating an unnecessary barrier between the people and God.[2] This public act of protest would have drawn

---

1. Matthew's parallels begin with a miraculous escape to avoid a wicked king who wanted to kill the infant Jesus (Matt 2:13–20), which mirrors baby Moses's miraculous escape from Pharaoh's death warrant (Exod 1:22—2:10), and continue on from there.

2. John places this incident near the beginning of his Gospel (John

The Jesus I Didn't Know I Didn't Know

attention to himself during the potentially volatile Passover week, and so provoked political and religious repercussions. And in the Synoptic Gospels, this incident follows Jesus's so-called triumphal entry into Jerusalem, when he rode into the city on a donkey—which was another politically charged act.

It was a mix of religion and politics that led to Jesus's arrest and trial. Jesus's enemies bring him to Governor Pontius Pilate, alluding to Jesus speaking about a "kingdom" as justification for the need of Roman justice. This explains the question Pilate asks of Jesus, "Are *you* the *king* of the Jews?"[3] Of course, we don't know his tone, but it was likely incredulous; how could this poor man from rural Palestine, and of no significant birth, be royalty! According to John, Jesus is not silent.[4] In fact, he responds eruditely: "My kingdom is not from this world."[5] This does not mean that Christ's kingdom is vague or purely spiritual; his kingdom is *for* the world, just not *from* it. Because Jesus's response mentions the word kingdom, Pilate replies, "So you are a king!"[6] But as the conversation continues, Pilate realizes the man in front of him is no threat to his power or to the Roman peace (*pax Romana*). If anything, Jesus is more of a poet or a philosopher than a politician. Pilate concludes, "I find no case against him," a phrase John and Luke have Pilate say three times in their accounts of the trial.[7] Throughout John's description of events leading to the crucifixion, the emphasis is on Jesus being the king of the Jews, which is obviously a political title. In the end, Pilate has a cynical notice

---

2:13–25), whereas the other Gospels have this occurring during Jesus's last week in Jerusalem (Mark 11:15–17; Matt 21:12–17; Luke 19:45–46).

3. Mark 15:2; Luke 23:3; Matt 27:11; John 18:33.

4. Matthew's and Luke's accounts say Jesus was silent before his accusers, no doubt alluding to Isa 53:7. See Matt 27:12, 14; Luke 23:9.

5. John 18:36.

6. John 18:37 NET.

7. John 18:38b; 19:4, 6b; Luke 23:4, 14, 22. This triple usage implies this point is unambiguous. John and Luke are emphasizing to their readers that Jesus's crucifixion was unjust because Pilate *knew* Jesus was innocent. Luke later reemphasizes this point through the words of one of the criminals who was crucified alongside Jesus. See Luke 23:41.

The Politics of Jesus

fastened to the cross and written in Aramaic, Latin, and Greek: "Jesus of Nazareth, the King of the Jews."[8]

When we hear the word kingdom, we think of a geographical region ruled by a monarch. Indeed, as mentioned before, a popular Jewish expectation of the messiah was of such a ruler overthrowing foreign oppression, restoring Israel's land and independent status in the world. Had that been Jesus's ambition, Pilate would have had no hesitation in killing him. I therefore think that Jesus's proclamation of a kingdom can be quite confusing. To make matters worse, Matthew (exclusively) speaks of the "kingdom of heaven" whereas the other New Testament writers speak of the "kingdom of God." Kingdom of heaven sounds otherworldly, even exclusively in the future—as a kingdom belonging to God's domain. However, a comparison of the parallel passages of Mark and Luke with those of Matthew makes it abundantly clear they are referring to the same thing. (Matthew is thought to have been using the word heaven to avoid using the holy—and unspoken—name of God, which would likely have offended devout Jewish readers.) For me it is simpler to speak only of the kingdom of God or the kingdom belonging to God. This aspect of certain things belonging to God is also illustrated in the trick question Jesus is asked: "Should Jews pay Imperial taxes?" Jesus shrewdly replies, "Give back to Caesar what is Caesar's and to God what is God's."[9] The point being that we are to live *in* this world, for we belong to it. Nevertheless, our prime loyalty is to God—not the state.[10]

Before talking more about the kingdom of God, it is worth stepping back to gain an overall view. Sometimes studying a theme or topic such as this is like a jigsaw puzzle; it is easier if we have the complete picture in front of us. New Testament scholars come to our aid here. Here is a viewpoint I have found to be helpful.

First-century Jews expected the present age to dramatically change into the age to come when the final judgment arrived, the

---

8. John 19:19–20; see also Matt 27:37; Mark 15:26; Luke 23:38.

9. See Mark 12:13–17; Matt 22:15–22; Luke 20:20–26. I appreciate this is taken slightly out of context, but not inappropriately.

10. While this is true, this statement somewhat trivializes Jesus's complex response to a loaded question. See also Matt 6:24.

The Jesus I Didn't Know I Didn't Know

so-called Day of the LORD. If a general resurrection of the dead was going to happen at all—and that concept was debated in Jesus' day[11]—it would happen only on the Day of the LORD. In light of the resurrection witnessed by his followers, the early church came to understand Jesus to be redefining that expectation. As with many things about Jesus, his bodily resurrection contributed to a paradigm shift in their thinking. The fact that he rose from the dead at that particular point in time could be explained only if the future Day of the LORD had somehow begun in the present. You will recall that Jesus, following John the Baptist, preached that the "kingdom of God has come near."[12] With the resurrection, God's kingdom had—in some sense—come. The Day of the LORD became, in effect, the Day of the Lord Jesus.[13] This being the case, the big picture is that God's reign has begun with Jesus—God decisively acted through him—and it is currently operating in parallel with this present age, as shown in Figure 1. This overlapping in time of the kingdom of God and the kingdom(s) of this world is often referred to as the "now and not yet" kingdom of God. I find this term helpful in two ways: it speaks of God's kingdom in the temporal domain, rather than the spatial,[14] and as having begun. However, the "not yet" indicates it's certainly not fully realized; evil is still very much present, impeding and interfering with God's kingdom.

---

11. In first-century Palestine, the influential Sadducees were the Jerusalem-based aristocracy of Judaism and included most of the leading priestly families. They only saw the Pentateuch, the first five books of the Old Testament, as authoritative and consequently were (at times) in disagreement with the Pharisees. For example, the Sadducees did not believe in the general resurrection, whereas the Pharisees did. See Mark 12:18–27; Matt 22:23–33.

12. Mark 1:15; Matt 3:2, 4:17. Luke 17:21 has "The kingdom of God is in your midst—or among you" NET, NIV, NRSV.

13. Paul uses this term in 1 Cor 1:8; 2 Cor 1:14; Phil 1:6, 10 but still as a future event, the return/coming of King Jesus.

14. This means God's reign does not recognize national boundaries. And there is no such thing as a *Christian* nation.

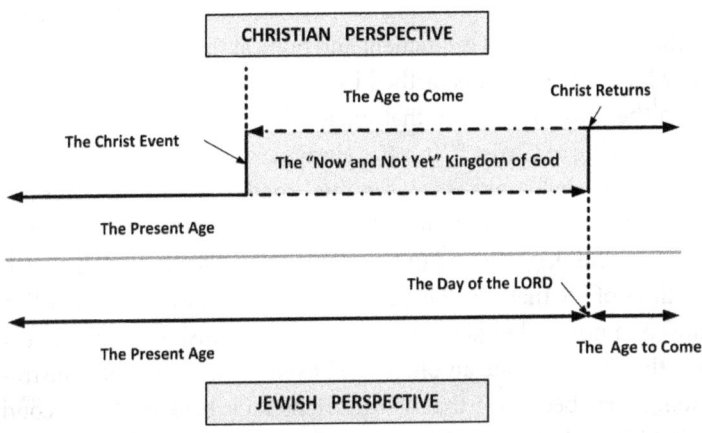

A Comparison of Jewish and Christian perspectives on the two ages or eras of history. With the birth-life-death-resurrection-ascension of Jesus the Messiah—the *Christ Event*—the early Christians saw the new age as having begun in the present. This is referred to here as the "now and not yet" kingdom (or reign) of God.

The broad New Testament panorama is then that when Christ returns, he will bring about the harvest—a common Jewish metaphor that includes the final judgment—and that is when evil will be completely destroyed and God's kingdom will come in all its fulness.[15] In Paul's language, the "new creation" has already begun, and we are to live confident that the "old creation" has no ultimate power over us.[16] That concept of the new creation arises because the resurrection of Jesus occurred on the first day of the week. As mentioned before, the ongoing week of new creation continues until the final Sabbath rest arrives, when Christ appears (his coming, Greek: *parousia*). This paradoxical notion of the now and not yet kingdom of God is also present in Paul's contrasting language of "life in the Spirit" and "life in the flesh."[17] Moreover, Paul recognized the continuing suffering in the world and speaks of us, along with the

15. See, for example, Matt 13:24–30, 36–43.
16. See 2 Cor 5:17.
17. See Rom 8:1–17. There is important theological meaning and nuance that needs to be explored in Romans 8.

The Jesus I Didn't Know I Didn't Know

whole of creation, as "groaning as in the pains of childbirth."[18] There is therefore a sense of excitement and hope at the future prospect of new life, but one that is birthed by pain and suffering—beginning with the cross. In light of that image, Paul writes of us sharing in the suffering of Christ.[19] This has always struck me as a bit weird or pretentious, but it makes sense in this broader context. And let's not forget that Jesus himself said, "Take up your cross and follow me."[20]

All this might sound unbelievable and, in the face of the harsh realities of life that we all experience, one might even consider this now and not yet kingdom of God to be mere wishful thinking. Let me therefore provide an often-cited example as a credible illustration. It has been said that as historians look back on the Second World War, the key turning point in Europe was the Allied landings in Normandy on June 6, 1944. This is not to belittle the earlier campaigns in North Africa or Italy, in which my father-in-law fought, nor the Northern Front in Russia. But something decisively new was needed if further progress was to be made in Europe. The Allies put a monumental amount of effort into the Normandy landings. If establishing and maintaining that beachhead succeeded, then a critical new battlefront could be opened up. If it failed, the Allies were doomed. The D-Day landings were very costly in terms of human life, but their success effectively guaranteed the ultimate victory—so historians say (with the benefit of hindsight). Of course, that did not mean that the war was over; many battles still followed. And no one knew *when* the war in Europe would end. Nevertheless, the final outcome was assured; it was only a matter of time. While no analogy is perfect, many have compared the beachhead landings in Normandy to Jesus inaugurating the now and not yet kingdom of God with his life, death, resurrection, and ascension. And because of his resurrection from the dead, Christians believe the ultimate defeat of evil is guaranteed, even though we still suffer hardship today with the ongoing effects of evil in its many forms.

---

18. See Rom 8:18–25 NIV.
19. See Phil 3:10; 2 Cor 1:5–7; Rom 8:17; see also 1 Pet 4:13.
20. Mark 8:34; Luke 9:23; 14:27; Matt 10:38; 16:24–26; see also John 16:33.

The Politics of Jesus

Once we recognize the overall picture, we can explore specific New Testament references to the kingdom of God—the individual pieces of the jigsaw puzzle—and begin to place things in context.

The first major unit on the ministry of Jesus in Matthew's Gospel is the Sermon on the Mount.[21] This explosive text is radical! It has been described as a manifesto of the kingdom—and using that word makes it *political* in the sense that it presents the agenda of God's reign. It is also a *religious* minefield, in that Matthew has Jesus as an authoritative Moses-like figure reinterpreting the Torah for those times. In whatever sense one hears it, such a message was—and is—bound to provoke a reaction. The sermon begins with a series of statements on blessedness known as the Beatitudes:[22]

> Blessed are the poor in spirit, for theirs is the kingdom of heaven.
> Blessed are those who mourn, for they will be comforted.
> Blessed are the meek, for they will inherit the earth.
> Blessed are those who hunger and thirst for righteousness, for they will be filled.
> Blessed are the merciful, for they will receive mercy.
> Blessed are the pure in heart, for they will see God.
> Blessed are the peacemakers, for they will be called children of God.
> Blessed are those who are persecuted for righteousness' sake, for theirs is the kingdom of heaven.
> Blessed are you when people revile you and persecute you and utter all kinds of evil against you falsely on my account. Rejoice and be glad, for your reward is great in heaven, for in the same way they persecuted the prophets who were before you.

If Pontius Pilate had witnessed such a speech, he would have roared with laughter. A king who promoted such a manifesto would be no threat to any tyrant whose rule was backed up with military force. There is simply no way the meek will inherit the earth! The poor in spirit (or the humble, or simply the poor in Luke's version) are people of no influence, then and now. Those who show mercy—or

---

21. Matt 5—7; Matthew follows this sermon with a unit on the *miracles* of Jesus (Matt 8—9) and later the *parables* of Jesus (Matt 13).

22. Matt 5:3-12. Compare with Luke 6:20-23. Luke's "blessings" are contrasted with "woes" (Luke 6:24-26); see also Matt 23:13-39.

The Jesus I Didn't Know I Didn't Know

those who forgive others—often get abused by others in return, rather than having their grace reciprocated. And those references to heaven and being called God's children all seem otherworldly—wishful pie in the sky when you die. It is too easy to dismiss these words as those of a naïve eccentric. What on earth did Jesus mean?

From the Beatitudes it is evident that the kingdom of God has upside down values in comparison to the power structures of this world. The quip "Remember the Golden Rule: the one with the gold makes the rules" is, alas, all too true. Those who are rich (or otherwise powerful) frequently build and control systems in such a way as to maintain and expand their wealth. Those systems are a complex mix—even to the extent of manipulation—of economics (including taxation) and human resources on local, national, and global scales. Moreover, and perhaps more significantly, rich "benefactors" influence political parties and lobbying groups through their donations—and such actions are often self-serving and symbiotic. Furthermore, economic sanctions and tariffs, sometimes coupled with military action, enable rich countries to maintain their wealth at the expense of the poor and vulnerable. That is the way the world works—and it's tragic. Just look at the consequences! Jesus, however, says that God's kingdom is nothing like that. It is not based on wealth, power, and influence. In fact, it is the very opposite. Jesus famously said, "It is easier for a camel to go through the eye of a needle than for someone who is rich to enter the kingdom of God."[23] (More on what that means in a moment.)

In the Beatitudes, Jesus says that it is the humble and poor who are a part of God's kingdom, along with those who are persecuted as a direct consequence of following God's ways. And those with integrity will see God; peacemakers also belong to God. God will exalt the meek and powerless,[24] and those who forgive others will themselves receive grace, for nothing is unnoticed by God![25] Those who mourn and suffer will not be forgotten but will receive

---

23. Mark 10:25; Luke 18:25; Matt 19:24.

24. See Matt 23:12; Luke 1:52–53; Prov 3:34; 29:23; Jas 4:6; 1 Pet 5:5.

25. That concept in repeated in the Lord's Prayer: "Forgive us our sins, for we also forgive everyone who sins against us," Luke 11:4 NIV; Matt 6:12. See also Sir 28:2–3, 7 (and chapter 4, page 31, footnote 19).

The Politics of Jesus

God's strength. And those who are honestly seeking for God, but are hindered or hurt by others (including the church), will be truly satisfied. Everyone who fits into those categories is designated as blessed or honored by God. Such people are the vulnerable, those often ignored, unappreciated, and even oppressed in society. Yet Jesus says God's kingdom is precisely for "the least of these."[26]

We need to appreciate that these words were equally shocking in Jesus's day. But words can be cheap unless followed up by action—and that is what Matthew relates in the subsequent chapters. Throughout all the Gospel accounts, Jesus is portrayed as socializing with the lowly, such as social outcasts, the sick, defenseless widows, and generally those whom devoutly religious people thought were unworthy of God's attention. For such associations Jesus was pejoratively labeled the "friend of 'sinners.'"[27] Why is all this so noteworthy? In my mind it's because we are still inclined to think that God has favorites, and they are stereotypically clean-living, upstanding citizens who are considered to be deeply religious. Yet near the end of the Sermon on the Mount, Jesus says: "Not everyone who says to me, 'Lord, Lord,' will enter the kingdom of heaven (or kingdom of God), but only the one who does the will of my Father in heaven."[28] This is stunning! Just saying we are Christians is not enough. Actions matter, humility matters, having integrity matters, living out kingdom values matters.[29]

Another reason these words are so revolutionary is because of the religious expectations of Jesus's day. Later in the sermon Jesus says, "You cannot serve both God and money."[30] This is also fleshed out in a conversation between Jesus and a rich young man.[31] At the conclusion, Jesus says to his disciples, "How hard it is for those who have wealth to enter the kingdom of God!" The disciples are

26. See Matt 25:31–46, esp. 40.
27. Matt 11:19.
28. Matt 7:21, see also Matt 25:10–12.
29. See also Matt 25:31–46.
30. Matt 6:24 NIV. See also 1 Tim 6:9–10; Mark 4:18–19; Matt 13:22; Luke 8:14. Having wealth is then a test of character and of responsibility, as to how a person uses it.
31. See Mark 10:17–31; Matt 19:16–22; Luke 18:18–30.

The Jesus I Didn't Know I Didn't Know

astonished at these words. Why would they be so surprised by that? Their amazement indicates that they shared the general Old Testament view that regarded wealth as a blessing from God, a sign of divine favor.[32] People naturally assumed that the wealthy elite were closer to God than were common people. Jesus, in the Beatitudes, redefines God's blessing in entirely different terms. Jesus turns that whole way of thinking upside down, and the disciples are astounded.

Jesus then says: "It is easier for a camel to go through the eye of a needle than for someone who is rich to enter the kingdom of God."[33] I remember at Sunday School being taught that the needle's eye referred to a small gate in the wall surrounding Jerusalem and that camels had to be completely unloaded before trying to squeeze through the entranceway on their knees. However convenient the image, there was no such gate in Jerusalem and this story first appeared in a ninth-century commentary on this passage.[34] This is a rationalization to soften the force of the text; it provides a possible route into the kingdom, on our knees and without the baggage of possessions. While that may be consistent with what Jesus asked the rich man to do—sell everything and give the money to the poor—it is not the meaning of the camel and the eye of the needle adage. No, this is a proverbial saying that shows the sheer impossibility of the action.[35] And the disciples are flabbergasted. They ask, "Who then can be saved?" or "Who then can enter the kingdom?" And Jesus replies: "For mortals it is impossible, but not for God; for God all things are possible."[36] This saying expresses again the fact that entry

32. See Deut 28:1–14; Job 1:10; 42:10; Prov 10:22. In the Greco-Roman world, as well as in the Jewish faith, material property was widely seen as a reward or a by-product of spiritual virtue. Today this has morphed into the prosperity gospel heresy.

33. Mark 10:25; Luke 18:25; Matt 19:24.

34. See Boring, *Mark*, 292.

35. In Jewish rabbinical literature, "an elephant passing through the eye of the needle" was a figure of speech for sheer impossibility. Another variant is to note the Greek for camel (*kamelon*) and a ship's mooring cable (*kamilon*) are very similar. To again help rationalize or soften this saying of Jesus, some have suggested the use of camel was therefore a copyist's error.

36. Mark 10:27. Nevertheless, "for God all things are possible" is expressed

into the kingdom is made possible only because of God's gracious initiative. For sure there are things we can and should do once we are part of God's kingdom,[37] but we cannot earn entry by those things and actions that our culture considers meritorious.

I want to pause for a moment to comment on what I didn't know I didn't know. Like most Protestants, I was raised on Paul's emphasis of being saved "by grace" (*sola gratia*). Martin Luther didn't like the book of James, calling it "an epistle of straw," for its perceived emphasis on salvation by works—meaning salvation that is merited by good deeds. Yet James has many parallels with Matthew's Gospel and all this can create a tension between Paul's Jesus and those of the Gospel writers.[38] Yet if we consider Matthew's account, we find that he carefully navigates between grace and works; both are essential.[39] I believe Paul would also agree. The above account of the camel and the needle's eye is one example that illustrates grace. Another example is Jesus's famous phrase, "Truly I tell you, unless you change and become like little children, you will never enter the kingdom."[40] Let's consider this statement briefly, as understanding what this saying means is vitally important for kingdom theology—and that's another thing I didn't know I didn't know.

On a different occasion Jesus powerfully enacts this upside down teaching of the kingdom of God with the help of a child.[41] The act of a religious teacher embracing a child in his arms is a culturally shocking thing for his male disciples to grasp. So, if we see this as a cuddly photo opportunity, like politicians kissing babies

---

here in the *context of salvation* itself (i.e., entry into the kingdom). It does not mean every miracle we ask for in prayer is therefore possible or likely. This complex, pastoral, and theological theme is explored in Reddish, *Does God Always Get What God Wants?*

37. See Matt 25:31–46.

38. This is elegantly examined in Dunn, *Jesus, Paul, and the Gospels*.

39. For example, see the parable of the workers in the vineyard (Matt 20:1–16) and Jesus's teaching on the sheep and the goats (Matt 25:31–46). Our attitude and actions in response to God's grace are also illustrated in the parable of the talents (Matt 25:14–30).

40. Matt 18:3–4; Mark 10:15; Luke 18:16–17. See also Matt 5:20.

41. See Mark 9:33–37; Matt 18:1–5.

The Jesus I Didn't Know I Didn't Know

during an election campaign, then we have completely missed the point. When our culture thinks of babies and young children, there is often a sentimental image of innocence. And even if young children become disruptive in public, we still assume they have individuality and dignity. But in the first-century Mediterranean world, children had no status nor legal rights.[42] They were utterly dependent upon their father, who could—if he so wished—easily disown them. To live in the kingdom of God, in this context, is to be utterly dependent upon the Father—upon God's grace, God's generosity—rather than on our own merit, or legal right, or a misplaced sense of personal entitlement. And Jesus enacts that grace by taking children into his arms and blessing them. Jesus's teaching concerning children is then not a lesson about being childlike, meaning innocence—or perhaps as having a simple, believing faith. No, he is speaking to the issue of status.[43] Since children were socially invisible in those days, what Jesus says next is equally astonishing: "Whoever welcomes one of these little children in my name welcomes me; and whoever welcomes me does not [only] welcome me but the one who sent me."[44] Jesus elevates the statusless child to be a stand-in for himself, and not just for himself—but for God. Powerful and thought-provoking words indeed!

Through these and other examples, Jesus acknowledges that *everyone* is made in the image of God.[45] There is more inclusivity in the kingdom of God than many devout people typically think. This is vividly portrayed in the parable of the good Samaritan in response to the pointed question, "Who is my neighbor?"[46] It is also the backdrop for Jesus's command to "Love your enemies" in the Sermon on the Mount.[47] We are to love people with whom we don't

---

42. See Gal 4:1–2. Romans who needed heirs commonly adopted adults rather than children.

43. After all, Jesus—and presumably God—would want us to develop a *mature* faith. See also 1 Cor 14:20; Phil 1:9–11; Col 1:28, 2:6–7; Eph 4:10–16; 2 Pet 1:5–9.

44. Mark 9:37 NIV; Matt 18:4–5.

45. Gen 1:26–27.

46. Luke 10:25–37.

47. Matt 5:44. Jesus is not being original here; he is reiterating Prov 25:21–22. See also Luke 6:27–36; 1 John 4:10–11.

get along and those of other faiths and ethnicities. Why? Because that is *precisely* what God does! To belong to God's kingdom means we are to do the same kinds of things God does. We are to love, reconcile, and forgive. And we are to be faithful, persistent, honest, generous, trusting, and discerning—for those are God's traits. And we are to put into practice all that Jesus taught and modelled for us. That's the politics of King Jesus: what a manifesto!

Chapter 7

The Temple of Jesus

I struggle with the concept of the omnipresence of God. Of all the classical attributes of God, you might think this one is the easiest to accept—or the least contentious. My concern may seem obscure or even obtuse to you, but the notion of omnipresence gives the impression that God is to be found equally anywhere or that the divine presence is uniform throughout creation. I suspect it follows from a classical understanding of omnipotence: God is deemed all-powerful, so nothing can stop God from being in all places at once. I certainly agree that there's no such thing as a no-go zone for God, but that does not mean his presence must be found *equally* in all places and times. I am not trying to be difficult or pedantic. In fact, I have biblical evidence to support my qualms. Please allow me to explain.

In the Old Testament, God's spirit is said to be only upon special people: judges, prophets, kings, and priests—and not even all of them! Kings and priests were hereditary roles, and not all of them followed in God's ways, meaning not all trusted in God and kept the covenant. More significantly, God's presence was to be found in special places, particularly the tabernacle and, later, the temple in Jerusalem.[1] Furthermore, at special times God's presence was incredibly potent (called a theophany), like in the

---

1. There were other places too, often marked by a shrine that memorialized a person's special encounter with God, e.g., Bethel (Gen 12:8; 35:1) and Ophrah (Judg 6:22–24).

The Temple of Jesus

burning bush incident that Moses experienced.[2] What this signifies to me is that the Jewish people understood God's presence to be in *particular* people, locations, and occasions. Moreover, the psalmist, the prophets, and the writer of Job understood the experiential silence of God. And this could even be interpreted as God's absence. This background context does not seem to justify the notion of divine omnipresence. I suggest this is more of a Greek idea than a Hebrew one.

In the New Testament, we find something changes. For example, Luke reports the Holy Spirit coming upon all kinds of people at Pentecost.[3] Peter saw this as a fulfilment of an oracle from the prophet Joel:

> In the last days, God says, I will pour out my Spirit on *all people*. Your sons and daughters will prophesy, your young men will see visions, your old men will dream dreams. Even on my servants, *both men and women*, I will pour out my Spirit in those days, and they will prophesy.[4]

This again points to God's generosity and inclusivity in his kingdom. Ordinary people will be filled with the divine spirit, young and old—not simply prophets, priests, and kings. How are we to understand this change in God's presence?

In the Old Testament, the prophet Ezekiel had a powerful vision of the divine spirit leaving the temple at the time of the Babylonian exile.[5] He later had another vision of God's glorious presence eventually returning to a restored temple.[6] We are told that God's presence would come from the east, the same direction from which it had departed earlier.[7] There is, however, no clear sense of this

---

2. See Exod 3.
3. See Acts 2.
4. Acts 2:17–18 NIV (italics added); Luke cites and adapts Joel 2:28–29. "All people" does not mean everybody, rather, all *kinds* of people. Later, in Acts 10, the Holy Spirit is dramatically bestowed upon non-Jews.
5. See Ezek 10–11.
6. Ezek 43:1–12.
7. Ezek 43:2; 10:19; 11:23.

The Jesus I Didn't Know I Didn't Know

vision being realized when the temple was rebuilt.[8] Understanding that background shapes how we read the Gospel accounts. Consider, for example, Jesus's entry into Jerusalem riding upon a donkey. This is related in all four Gospels with geographic detail and with many references and allusions to the Old Testament Scriptures.[9] Moreover, the Gospel writers then describe the many activities of Jesus in the temple area during that Passover week. The point being that when Jesus entered (and exited) Jerusalem, via the Mount of Olives—with its magnificent view of the temple—he was approaching the city *from the east*. I suggest this is a noteworthy, literary hint that pertains to the presence of God.

After Jesus's famous altercation in the temple forecourt, where he overturns the money changers' tables,[10] John gives his account and commentary on events:

> Jesus replied, "Destroy this temple and in three days I will raise it up again." Then the Jewish leaders said to him, "This temple has been under construction for forty-six years, and are you going to raise it up in three days?" *But Jesus was speaking about the temple of his body.* So after he was raised from the dead, his disciples remembered that he had said this, and they believed the scripture and the saying that Jesus had spoken.[11]

Jesus had apparently mentioned the future destruction of the temple before[12]—and it *was* later destroyed in 70 CE. As an aside, it is worth noting that at least three of the four biblical Gospels were

---

8. See Ezra 6:13–18.

9. See Mark 11:1–11; Matt 21:1–11; Luke 19:28–44; John 12:12–19. See also Zech 9:9–10; 14:4.

10. See Mark 11:15–18; Matt 21:12–13; Luke 19:45–46; John 2:14–16.

11. John 2:19–22 NET (italics added). Furthermore, in Matt 12:6, Jesus, in the context of him (the Son of Man) being the Lord of the Sabbath, says: "I tell you, something greater than the temple is here." This also connects with the claim "the Son of Man has authority on earth to forgive sins" (Mark 2:10; Matt 9:6; Luke 5:24). Such a claim challenges the traditional function of the temple itself, with its sacrifices for the forgiveness of sin.

12. See Mark 13:1–2; 14:58; 15:29; Matt 24:2; 26:60–61; 27:40; Luke 21:5–6; Acts 6:14.

The Temple of Jesus

written after 70 CE, and that cataclysmic event changed the Jewish religious landscape forever. This tragedy influenced the Gospel writers and their Christian communities too. The destruction of the temple was therefore understood to have *theological* significance. John also reports a conversation with a Samaritan woman at a well, one which included the contentious issue as to where was the appropriate place to worship God.[13] (The Samaritans worshiped God on their holy Mount Gerizim, whereas the Jews worshiped God at the temple in Jerusalem.) Jesus responds by saying that soon—indeed the time is at hand—the location of God's (assumed) presence will be irrelevant:

> But a time is coming—and now is here—when the true worshipers will worship the Father in spirit and truth, for the Father seeks such people to be his worshipers. God is spirit, and the people who worship him must worship in spirit and truth.[14]

Implicit in this text is that this coming time or new era has arrived in the person of Jesus himself. This conversation with the woman from Samaria is another example of inclusivity and ties in with the significance of the first Pentecost mentioned above. It also affirms that God can be worshipped anywhere and is not restricted to traditional holy sites. But there is more...

John, in saying "But Jesus was speaking about the temple of his body,"[15] understood the divine presence to be embodied in Jesus the Messiah. Consequently, the locus of worship was no longer the temple in Jerusalem but in Jesus himself; in other words, no longer in a *place* but in a *person*. Earlier in his prologue, John writes: "Now the Word became flesh and took up residence among us. We saw his glory—the glory of the one and only, full of grace and truth, who came from the Father."[16] The "took up residence" phrase is literally "tabernacled" in Greek and alludes to where the *shekinah*—the

---

13. See John 4:1–42, esp. 19–26.
14. John 4:23–24 NET. See also Acts 7:48–50, citing Isa 66:1–2.
15. See John 2:21.
16. John 1:14 NET. See also John 1:18; Zech 2:10–11.

The Jesus I Didn't Know I Didn't Know

visible glory of God's presence—resided.[17] The implication being that the divine glory is now to be seen in Jesus, and they had witnessed it! This is radical thinking, and John tells us that the disciples' *aha* moment of understanding occurred sometime after the resurrection. As I have said before, the bodily resurrection of Jesus forced his followers to rethink who Jesus was—and is—in light of God's action in raising Jesus from the dead. His earlier cryptic comments began to make more sense as the Holy Spirit revealed the ongoing truth about Jesus to them.[18] I believe John's insight is profound. Nevertheless, is this perspective unique to John? No, as we will see below, the notion of God's presence being in a human temple is also implied in Paul's writings, and we can discern this idea of God's glory residing uniquely in Jesus in the Synoptic Gospels too.

If Jesus is the new temple, what happened after the ascension? Paul regards the church as the "body of Christ"[19] and that makes the church the new temple—the place where God's Spirit resides.[20] Paul, or possibly one of his associates, writes:

> You have been built on the foundation of the apostles and prophets, with Christ Jesus himself as the cornerstone. In him the whole building, being joined together, *grows into a holy temple in the Lord*, in whom you also are being built together into *a dwelling place of God in the Spirit*.[21]

This powerful image is both an honor and a daunting responsibility, and the church has not always lived up to this high calling. What I find particularly interesting is that Paul's understanding was developed *before* the destruction of the physical temple in Jerusalem.

---

17. See Exod 40:34-38; 1 Kgs 8:10-11. The tabernacle was the portable tent of meeting prior to the temple.

18. See John 14:25-26; 16:13-14.

19. See 1 Cor 12:13, 27; Rom 12:4; Col 1:18, 24.

20. The Holy Spirit dwells in the church, but not exclusively so, nor is the Spirit the prerogative of the church. The Spirit is always going *ahead* of the church in God's mission (*missio Dei*); we see this in Acts 10 and on Paul's missionary journeys.

21. Eph 2:20-22 NET (italics added); note the "you" here is plural. See also 1 Cor 3:16, 6:15a; 2 Cor 6:16 (along with Lev 26:12; Jer 32:38; Ezek 37:27); and 1 Pet 2:5.

The Temple of Jesus

Returning to the theme of God's glory residing in a person, the Synoptic Gospels each vividly describe the transfiguration of Jesus, which can be interpreted as an overwhelming enactment that reveals Jesus in divine glory.[22] To understand the transfiguration in a literary context, we need to appreciate what this story would have meant to Jews and non-Jews at that time. This description is rooted in Greek traditions about gods walking the earth in human form and manifesting their divine glory or radiance. This Hellenistic notion is adapted to Hebrew accounts of theophany, where God vividly reveals Godself in the Old Testament. One such example occurred when Moses went up Mount Sinai, which was covered in cloud—symbolizing the presence of God. When Moses later appeared out of the cloud, his face shone brightly and the Israelites were afraid to come near him; he therefore had to cover his face with a veil.[23] As I mentioned earlier, the Old Testament writers knew that God's presence was not uniform, but could occur with heightened intensity on rare, special occasions. In such instances—whether they were in a burning bush, a cloud, a whirlwind, or a still small voice—the divine presence was not fleeting, but intense and personal. Consider too the vision of Jacob's ladder, when the veil of the ordinariness that normally prevents us from seeing God at work was drawn back and a fuller reality of what God is doing in the world was disclosed.[24]

What, then, was the deeper reality being revealed in the transfiguration? The connection with Moses and Elijah reveals that Jesus is completing the work begun by the great lawgiver Moses and Israel's great prophet Elijah. Moses and Elijah were vital in preparing the way; Jesus is finishing the task. It also reveals that Jesus is not Moses or Elijah, but he is worthy of being in such exalted company.[25] Yet there is more than just a connection with these two past

---

22. See Mark 9:2–8; Matt 17:1–8; Luke 9:28–36. The transfiguration is also mentioned in 2 Pet 1:16–18. One can also interpret the accounts of Jesus walking on the water as a similar epiphany; see Mark 6:45–52; Matt 14:22–33; John 6:16–21. See also John 12:28–30.

23. Exod 24:15–18; 34:29–35.

24. Gen 28:10–19. This link is also important in understanding John 1:51.

25. Incidentally, Elijah was thought never to have died and was taken

The Jesus I Didn't Know I Didn't Know

heroes of faith. There is also an allusion to the future coming of the Son of Man in all his glory, when he comes to judge the nations.[26] This is signified in the bright clothes that Jesus wears, which further indicate that Jesus himself belongs to the divine domain. So while the language uses Old Testament imagery, the vision of Jesus in glory is also a glimpse of the future in the present.

We are then told, "A cloud appeared and covered them, and a voice came from the cloud: 'This is my Son, whom I love. Listen to him!'"[27] First, this affirmation is the one heard at Jesus's baptism, so identifying Jesus as the Messiah and coming King. Second, this is witnessed by Peter, James, and John on this occasion. Third, the emphatic "Listen to him" not only verifies Jesus's divine authority, it echoes the words attributed to Moses, "The LORD your God will raise up for you a prophet like me from among you, from your fellow Israelites. You must listen to him."[28]

It is also worth noting that Matthew, Mark, and Luke each sandwich the transfiguration between two incidents in which Jesus predicts his death and resurrection. On each occasion the disciples demonstrate their inability to accept that the Messiah will suffer and die before being raised in glory. This would be in contradiction to all messianic expectations and what they understood the kingdom of God to be. The moment of transfiguration, then, only sharpens the paradox with the unthinkable scandal of the cross. Not only does God's own beloved Son die, but his death is at the hands of those he came to save. This witnessed transformation and glorification of Jesus not only speaks to the identity of Jesus, but the Gospel writers—with the benefit of hindsight—then point out to their readers that Jesus will enter into his glory through rejection, suffering, and death. Those readers, living as they did around the time of the destruction of Jerusalem in 70 CE, may have been

---

directly to heaven in a chariot of fire (see 2 Kgs 2:1–15). There were also Jewish legends in Jesus's day that claimed Moses himself never died in the wilderness, since the location of his tomb was unknown (see Deut 34:6).

26. See Dan 7:13–14 and the discussion concerning the Son of Man in chapter 4. Concerning the role of Jesus as judge, see chapter 5, page 43, footnote 29.

27. Mark 9:7 NIV; Matt 17:5; Luke 9:35.

28. Deut 18:15 NIV.

The Temple of Jesus

encouraged by this account of the transfiguration as evidence of a now exalted Jesus. It demonstrated that the kingdom Jesus had been proclaiming was actually being implemented, despite the terrible violence and chaos they were experiencing. Christians today frequently think of Jesus in terms of heavenly glory or the triumph of Christ's (second) coming. Yet the Son of Man's glorification had three stages of elevation, so to speak: his being *lifted up* on the cross, his being *raised* from the dead, and his *ascending* to be with God the Father. Let's not focus solely on the last two and overlook the real presence of God on the cross. We tend to think that Jesus is most clearly revealed as the glorious Son of God in the resurrection and ascension rather than in the suffering. This transfiguration sandwich challenges us to revise our understanding of how God's presence is revealed in the world.

In conclusion, the temple of Jesus is a powerful image of God's new modus operandi. The risen Jesus passes on his authority to the church[29] and, using Paul's language, the collective body of the church is now the temple of the Holy Spirit. This being the case, the church is where you would (at least) expect to find the divine presence today. However, my original concern over the omnipresence of God remains because God's presence is still to be found, so it seems to me, non-uniformly in certain places and times—though now within and among ordinary people. And I find that latter aspect to be most inspiring. Put a different way, we live in the now and not yet kingdom of God; only when God's reign comes in all its fullness will we truly experience God's omnipresence.

---

29. See John 20:21–23; Matt 28:18–20; Luke 24:45–49.

Chapter 8

The Supremacy of Jesus

Let's be frank here: many people—including Christians—struggle with the church's doctrine of the Trinity. It *is* confusing. We say God is One and then we say God is Father, Son, and Holy Spirit, and that does not sound particularly logical. It *is* strange that the church's orthodox doctrines and traditional creeds stress the Triune God. One of the differences between the Eastern Orthodox Church and the Western Church has been over nuanced meanings of the Trinity. In the Latin West, we have stressed the oneness of God first, with the trinitarian aspect added on like a thin veneer; the Greek East have the emphasis the other way around. Moreover, in our Western heritage, with the rise of science and the Enlightenment during the 1700s and 1800s, the Trinity essentially became fragmented. God became the distant Creator,[1] Jesus was reduced to a good moral teacher, and the embarrassing Holy Ghost of the King James Bible was largely forgotten or seen as impersonal.[2] The influential Roman Catholic theologian Karl Rahner was right to lament: "Despite their

---

1. As in deism.

2. In Greek, spirit (*pneuma*) is gender-neutral (neuter) and consequently some claim that as evidence for the Holy Spirit being impersonal. However, the Greek word for (prepubescent) child (*teknon*) is also neuter. Now while it is true that children were effectively regarded as the property of the head of the house, we today would certainly say children are persons! It is nevertheless fair to say that the divine spirit is not presented as a person in the Old Testament. The biblical writers' understanding of God is not fixed but develops with time, as does theology itself.

The Supremacy of Jesus

orthodox confession of the Trinity, Christians are, in their practical life, almost mere 'monotheists.'"[3] The emergence of a rationalized faith,[4] one which decries mystery in the divine life, still influences Christian thinking today. However, let's avoid the pitfall of imagining God to be in our own image, for such a god is no God at all but a puppet or an idol. The doctrine of the Trinity is, after all, a confessional statement of faith. It is not something we can prove, and it reminds us that there will always be an element of mystery to God.

Now it is true that the word Trinity is not to be found in the Bible.[5] But that does not mean it's a completely foreign idea to the New Testament. For example, Paul signs off his second letter to the Corinthians with the well-known benediction, "The grace of the Lord Jesus Christ and the love of God and the fellowship of the Holy Spirit be with you all."[6] And at the end of Matthew's Gospel, the risen Jesus says:

> All authority in heaven and on earth has been given to me. Go therefore and make disciples of all nations, baptizing them in the name of the Father and of the Son and of the Holy Spirit, and teaching them to obey everything that I have commanded you. And remember, I am with you always, to the end of the age.[7]

3. Rahner, *Trinity*, 10.

4. In other words, and speaking somewhat loosely, a merger of rationalism and Christianity.

5. Trinity was a term invented by Tertullian (ca. 160–225 CE).

6. 2 Cor 13:13 NET. This letter is thought to been written in about 56 CE. Other New Testament references that have Father, Son, and Spirit mentioned in close proximity are 1 Cor 12:4–6; 2 Cor 1:21–22; 1 Pet 1:2; Eph 4:4–6; Rev 1:4–5.

7. Matt 28:18–20. Note that this trinitarian baptismal formula is also in the *Didache* (Richardson, ed.), 7.1, and was possibly written before Matthew's Gospel, which itself is thought to have been written about 80–90 CE. Matthew also uses the phrase "in the name of," which means "in the authority of" (the Father, Son, and Holy Spirit). Incidentally, the phrase "I am with you always, to the end of the age" needs to be compared with the parting words of Moses: "For the LORD your God goes with you; he will never leave you nor forsake you," Deut 31:6 NIV; see also Josh 1:9. The key difference is that Jesus substitutes "the LORD" with *himself*, which makes sense only in light of the earlier sentence: "All authority in heaven and on earth has been given to me."

75

The Jesus I Didn't Know I Didn't Know

For both Paul and Matthew, the Father, Son, and Holy Spirit were all linked together, and evidently their audiences understood their collective importance in the liturgical life of the church. From texts like these, the Spirit is being implicitly presented as a person, rather than a force field or an energy source. The Spirit's traditional role is to make holy the people of God and sustain all of creation.[8] There are other passages that suggest the Spirit is personal too. Perhaps this is most notable in John's Gospel, where Jesus says to his followers,

> I will ask the Father, and he will give you another Advocate, to be with you forever. This is the Spirit of truth, whom the world cannot receive, because it neither sees him nor knows him. You know him, because he abides with you, and he will be in you.[9]

The Spirit here is said to be another Advocate or Comforter, because Jesus is the first Advocate.[10]

The New Testament has much more to say about the relationship between Jesus and God the Father, as discussed in chapter 5. Put bluntly, in the decades that followed the resurrection, followers of the risen Christ came to believe that Jesus was intimately and uniquely connected with God, in fact, God *enfleshed*. Those today who just want Jesus to be a good teacher find this uncomfortable—even offensive. What I didn't know I didn't know was there are far more hints in the New Testament that point to the divinity of Jesus than I had previously thought. Indeed, some are quite blatant when you consider the meaning of words and of titles, as this review has shown. Now this is a disturbing matter for religious moralists because, in our pluralistic society of many faiths, interfaith dialogue would be a much easier task if we could simply forget the notion of the divinity of Christ. Some Christians dilute or even deny their creedal tradition and go down that route. But we

---

8. Father, Son, and Holy Spirit are traditionally described as Creator, Redeemer, and Sanctifier (or Sustainer). A more nuanced understanding takes these roles as not exclusive to each person, for the Trinity's persons are not in isolation from each other but indwell (Greek: *perichoresis*) each other.

9. John 14:16–17. See also John 14:26; 15:26; 16:7–11.

10. See also Rom 8:26, 34; 1 John 2:1. Both Jesus and the Spirit are interceding on our behalf to God, but from different locations.

The Supremacy of Jesus

shouldn't be embarrassed about Christian truth claims, not least because those of other faiths and worldviews are not shy about their own. We are called to be authentic to our own beliefs while graciously dialoguing with those holding other views in order to further mutual understanding. Through this process we will identify where our values genuinely overlap and, by doing that, we can work together to enhance the broader society to which we belong. Sadly, too many Christians want to weaponize Jesus with reference to his divinity. The Jesus of the Gospels would decry such abuse.[11] With that said, in this final chapter, I want to now focus on the supremacy of Christ.

Col 1:15-20 is thought to be a very early hymn, similar to a confession of faith, and one that the writer cites because of its familiarity to his audience:[12]

> He is the image of the invisible God, the firstborn of all creation; for in him all things in heaven and on earth were created, things visible and invisible, whether thrones or dominions or rulers or powers—all things have been created through him and for him. He himself is before all things, and in him all things hold together. He is the head of the body, the church; he is the beginning, the firstborn from the dead, so that he might come to have first place in everything. For in him all the fullness of God was pleased to dwell, and through him God was pleased to reconcile to himself all things, whether on earth or in heaven, by making peace through the blood of his cross.

The author of Colossians is stressing a key theme in this letter, namely the centrality and supremacy of Jesus the Messiah. The hymn begins: "He [Messiah Jesus] is the image of the invisible

---

11. See also 1 Pet 3:15-16 NIV, keeping in mind the last clause: "Always be prepared to give an answer to everyone who asks you to give the reason for the hope that you have. But do this *with gentleness and respect*" (italics added).

12. Col 1:15-20, there is much that can be explored concerning a Greco-Roman appreciation of this poem in light of various philosophical worldviews of the time. Note that a confession of faith cannot be proved; by definition, a confession is a communal statement that begins, "We *believe* . . ." Another example of an early liturgical hymn is Phil 2:6-11.

The Jesus I Didn't Know I Didn't Know

God."[13] Christians have often said that if you want to know what God is like, look at Jesus, because he makes the invisible God visible. That's the first reason Jesus is supreme, because he is not a copy in the mere likeness of God, but the embodiment of God in our world. In case we fail to get it the first time, the author repeats this claim twice more: "For in Christ all the fullness of the Deity lives in bodily form."[14] Moreover, the writer of the book of Hebrews says the same thing: "The Son is the radiance of God's glory and the exact representation of his being."[15] Jesus is not then a demigod—half-divine, half-human. Jesus does not have a human body together with the divine spirit or mind. According to these writers, he can only be properly understood as a human being who literally embodies or incarnates the fullness of the one true God. Wow!

The hymn continues: "[Jesus] is the firstborn over all creation."[16] The word firstborn is repeated in the second stanza, and this word has created much controversy and debate in church history. By taking it literally, some today,[17] like the Arians of the fourth century,[18] use this text to claim Jesus is not co-eternal with God. In other words, Jesus was created—like an archangel. But firstborn can also mean of preeminent rank or supreme,[19] in this case over all creation, as the verse goes on to explain. Moreover, taking firstborn literally contradicts what immediately follows:

13. Col 1:15a. "He" refers to our "Lord Jesus Christ" (1:3) or "Christ Jesus" (1:4) and later "beloved Son" (1:13). Moreover, the analogy of image (Greek: *ikon*) implies a reflective mirror—polished metal surfaces in those days.

14. Col 2:9; 1:19 NIV.

15. Heb 1:3 NIV. It continues: "sustaining *all things* by his powerful word" (italics added). See also 2 Cor 4:4-6. (See Heb 1:1—3:6 for Christ being superior to the angels.)

16. Col 1:15b.

17. For example, Jehovah's Witnesses.

18. For the famous Arian controversy, see: Chadwick, *Early Church*, 133-51; Noll, *Turning Points*, 39-57.

19. See Ps 89:27 NIV, with reference to King David: "I will appoint him to be my firstborn, *the most exalted of the kings of the earth*" (italics added). It is therefore simply a mistake to think firstborn can mean only eldest child. Furthermore, it is unlikely that the subtleties of such temporal logic were in the writer of Colossians' thinking; such issues arose later.

The Supremacy of Jesus

For *in him* [that is, in Jesus] *all things* in heaven and on earth were created, things visible and invisible, whether thrones or dominions or rulers or powers—*all things* have been created *through him* and *for him*. He himself is *before all things*, and *in him all things* hold together.[20]

The repeated stress on all things is evident. An influential Church Father, Athanasius (c. 296–373 CE), was quick to point that out: "If all the creatures were created in him, he [Jesus] is *other* than the creatures, and he is *not* a creature, but the creator of the creatures."[21] Indeed, Jesus is described as the creator, the cohesion, and the culmination of all that is. This language may be poetic but the spirit of it is very clear, because such words are associated only with the divine. As we saw earlier in chapter 4, this is echoed in the opening of John's Gospel:

In the beginning was the Word, and the Word was with God, and the Word was God. He was in the beginning with God. *All things* came into being through him, and without him not one thing came into being. . . . And the Word became flesh and lived among us.[22]

The first-century writers saw no major inconsistency here with their Jewish tradition, but for sure they were adapting it.[23] What was it that led them to such grand conclusions?

The answer is in the second part of the hymn, which goes on to say: "[Messiah Jesus] is the head of the body, the church;[24] he is the beginning, the firstborn from the dead, so that he might come

---

20. Col 1:16–17 (italics added).
21. Cited in Lincoln, "Letter to the Colossians," 598 (italics added).
22. John 1:1–3, 14 (italics added).
23. See also 1 Cor 8:6; 2 Cor 8:9. Many have recognized the Old Testament picture of wisdom personified (see Prov 3:19–20; 8:22–36; Sir 24:8–9; Wis 7:24–28) and that she was created by God at the beginning. However, the stress here on creating "all things"—including "whether visible or invisible, whether thrones or dominions, whether principalities or powers"—suggests a Christology that is superior even to personified wisdom, particularly in light of "for him" (Col 1:16) and "in him" (Col 1:17).
24. Paul also uses the body image for the church in Rom 12:4–5; 1 Cor 10:16–17; 12:12–27.

The Jesus I Didn't Know I Didn't Know

to have first place in everything."[25] The use of the words head and firstborn again points to Christ's supremacy. Jesus is not only the world's creator; he is also the world's savior. "Firstborn from the dead" means simply the resurrection and points to Jesus being undisputedly preeminent over the new creation as well as the old.[26] It seems to me that the only plausible explanation for this hymn's confident proclamation of the Messiah's supremacy is the church's witness to the bodily resurrection of Jesus.

The hymn concludes by repeating its main confession of faith, followed by a succinct summary as to why is important. In short, it explains that the purpose of Christ's authority is for the benefit of the whole world:

> For in [Jesus] *all the fullness of God was pleased to dwell*, and *through him* God was pleased *to reconcile to himself all things*, whether on earth or in heaven, by making peace through the blood of his cross.[27]

Jesus, God in the flesh, is in the redeeming and reconciling business, and that is good news for everybody. This tells us of our worth to God—and that of the whole creation. All things are worth rescuing! Our rightful response is therefore one of gratitude. And we are reminded that this rescue package came through the cross, through suffering love. Yes, the world is full of ugliness and evil—including white privilege, as Black Lives Matter has recently brought to the foreground. Yet creation is also full of beauty and a source of joy, not just sadness, bitterness, and suffering. Jesus, God in human form, came to experience and absorb all of that evil in himself and be the source of healing for our broken world. In him we discover what true humanness entails in practice. That's why we need to appreciate that we are, in fact, integrated physical and spiritual beings. Those two notions are meant to be harmoniously united as one—and if we try to extract one from the other or deny the existence of the spiritual, we will never be able to address the complex social issues that we face. That's also why our faith is not a private

---

25. Col 1:18.
26. See also 1 Cor 15:20; Rom 8:29b; Rev 1:5.
27. Col 1:19–20 (italics added).

The Supremacy of Jesus

or an escapist spirituality cut off from the physical world around us. Rather, our faith in Jesus is to show the whole world what it means to be fully human and fully alive.

As I conclude, let me make two final observations. First, the doctrine of the Trinity is not then a mere addition made by a group of men centuries after Jesus lived, as if it were a conspiracy theory or some sort of fake news. As this study has demonstrated, the writers of the New Testament, each in their different way, address the "Who is Jesus?" question. I agree, the doctrine of the Trinity *is* perplexing. Nevertheless, I believe it is still a faithful summary/conclusion of all the New Testament texts concerning the identity of Jesus. Put a different way, it represents the trajectory of Scripture. Second, the writer of Colossians was quoting the hymn to make a point: belief in the supremacy of Jesus over all things has consequences. The author is asking his readers, "Do you understand what you are singing?" Jesus being preeminent—even preexistent—implies he is the one who has a rightful and unparalleled claim on our lives and on this world. Consequently, the writer goes on to warn us: "Be careful not to allow anyone to captivate you through an empty, deceitful philosophy that is according to human traditions . . . and not according to Christ."[28] Instead, he writes,

> Just as you received Christ Jesus as (supreme) Lord, continue to live your lives in him, rooted and built up in him and firm in your faith just as you were taught, and overflowing with thankfulness.[29]

With the Spirit of truth's help, may we all continue steadfast in this faith.

---

28. Col 2:8 NET. I omit "and the elemental spirits of the world" for simplicity.

29. Col 2:6–7 NET. The supreme is implied in the nuanced meaning of Lord, as discussed in chapter 4.

[Aslan said,] "Remember, remember, remember the signs. . . . Here on the mountain I have spoken to you clearly: I will not often do so down in Narnia. Here on the mountain, the air is clear and your mind is clear; as you drop down into Narnia, the air will thicken. Take great care that it does not confuse your mind. And the signs which you have learned here will not look at all as you expect them to look, when you meet them there. That is why it is so important to know them by heart and pay no attention to appearances. Remember the signs and believe the signs. Nothing else matters."[30]

30. Lewis, *Silver Chair*, 27.

Afterword

The older I get, the more I discover about Jesus that I didn't know I didn't know. I expect this to continue. There is more I could write about, such as on the sufferings of Jesus and his identity as the suffering Messiah. Or on the miracles of Jesus and the parables of Jesus and what they imply. While I see new things in these accounts each time I study them, these topics are perhaps more well-known.

In the Synoptic Gospels, we read that Jesus asks his followers a leading question: "Who do people say that I am?"[1] They reply that the people saw Jesus as a prophet, possibly the expected Elijah figure who would come before the messiah. (As mentioned in chapter 2, the Gospel writers saw John the Baptist as that Elijah figure.) We can ask the same question today and people might reply: a prophet, a holy man, a religious teacher, or some other description that implies he is one amongst many. Jesus then asks his closest followers, "But who do you say that I am?" And Peter answers him, "You are the Christ (or Messiah)." There is *uniqueness* in the title Messiah; Peter recognized that fact. In Matthew's version, Jesus tells Peter that he didn't discover that by human intuition or logic; rather God revealed that insight to him.[2]

At the end of John's Gospel, we read:

> Now Jesus performed many other miraculous signs in the presence of the disciples, which are not recorded in this book. But these are recorded so that you may believe

---

1. See Mark 8:27–30; Matt 16:13–20; Luke 9:18–20.
2. See Matt 16:16–19.

The Jesus I Didn't Know I Didn't Know

that Jesus is the Christ, the Son of God, and that by believing you may have life in his name.³

Again, we read of this emphasis on the identity of Jesus as the Messiah, God's Anointed One. But more than that, John's agenda in his organization of material is made explicit: "that you may believe." The Greek word for believe can also be translated "trust," and trust is ongoing, risky, and active—not merely intellectual assent. John also wanted his readers to discover that Jesus is the source of life!

It seems to me that the "Who do you say that I am" question is a timeless one. A book like this one provides an initial basis to consider when responding to it. While a rational case for the identity of Jesus can be made, in the final analysis, we are invited to learn to trust in the risen and glorified Jesus Christ.

What about Jesus didn't *you* know you didn't know? One could say that's a redundant question: if someone knew the answer, they would already know! Nevertheless, regardless of what you previously knew about Jesus, I hope your ongoing journey of discovery was stimulated and enhanced by these biblical reflections on the identity of Jesus.

3. John 20:30–31 NET.

ANOTHER EARLY CONFESSIONAL HYMN

Messiah Jesus, who though he existed in the form of God
did not regard equality with God as something to be grasped,
but emptied himself by taking on the form of a slave,
by looking like other men, and by sharing in human nature.
He humbled himself, by becoming obedient to the point of
death—even death on a cross!
As a result, God highly exalted him and gave him the name
that is above every name,
so that at the name of Jesus every knee will bow
—in heaven and on earth and under the earth—
and every tongue confess that Jesus Christ is Lord
to the glory of God the Father.

PHIL 2:6–11 (NET)
(WRITTEN BEFORE THE GOSPELS)

Bibliography

COMMENTARY SERIES AND BIBLES

Attridge, Harold W., ed. *HarperCollins Study Bible: New Revised Standard Version, including Apocryphal Deuterocanonical Books with Concordance.* Rev. ed. New York: HarperCollins, 2006.

Barclay, William. *The New Daily Study Bible.* 17 vols. Louisville: Westminster John Knox, 2001–2004.

Bartlett, David L., and Barbara Brown Taylor, eds. *Feasting on the Word.* 12 vols. Louisville: Westminster John Knox, 2008–2011.

Berlin, Adele, and Marc Zvi Brettler, eds. *Jewish Study Bible.* Oxford: Oxford University Press, 2004.

Jarvis, Cynthia A., and E. Elizabeth Johnson, eds. *Feasting on the Gospels.* 7 vols. Louisville: Westminster John Knox, 2015.

Keck, Leander E., ed. *New Interpreter's Bible Commentary.* 12 vols. Nashville: Abingdon, 1994–2004.

Mays, James Luther, and Paul J. Achtmeier, eds. *Interpretation: A Bible Commentary for Teaching and Preaching.* New Testament. 17 vols. Louisville: Westminster John Knox, 1982–1997.

New English Translation Bible. 1st ed. Dallas: Biblical Studies Press, 2005. www.netbible.com.

Pietersma, Albert, and Benjamin G. Wright, eds. *A New English Translation of the Septuagint.* Oxford: Oxford University Press, 2007.

Wright, N. T. *New Testament for Everyone.* 18 vols. Louisville: Westminster John Knox, 2001–2011.

Bibliography

BOOKS

Bailey, Kenneth E. *Jesus through Middle Eastern Eyes: Cultural Studies in the Gospels*. Downers Grove, IL: InterVarsity, 2008.
Beilby, James K., and Paul R. Eddy. *The Historical Jesus: Five Views*. Downers Grove, IL: InterVarsity, 2009.
Black, C. Clifton. *Mark*. Nashville: Abingdon, 2011.
Blomberg, Craig L. *The Historical Reliability of the Gospels*. 2nd ed. Downers Grove, IL: InterVarsity, 2007.
———. *Jesus and the Gospels: An Introduction and Survey*. 2nd ed. Nashville: B & H, 2009.
Borg, Marcus J. *Meeting Jesus Again for the First Time*. New York: HarperCollins, 1994.
Borg, Marcus J., and N. T. Wright. *The Meaning of Jesus: Two Visions*. New York: HarperCollins, 2007.
Boring, M. Eugene. *An Introduction to The New Testament: Literature, History, Theology*. Louisville: Westminster John Knox, 2012.
———. *Mark: A Commentary*. Louisville: Westminster John Knox, 2006.
Branick, Vincent P. *Understanding the Prophets and Their Books*. Mahwah, NJ: Paulist, 2012.
Brown, Raymond E. *Christ in the Gospels of the Liturgical Year*. Collegeville, MN: Liturgical, 2008.
———. *An Introduction to The New Testament*. New Haven: Yale University Press, 1997.
Bruce, F. F. *Jesus: Lord and Savior*. Downers Grove, IL: InterVarsity, 1986.
Chadwick, Henry. *The Early Church*. Rev. ed. Penguin History of the Church 1. London: Penguin, 1993.
Charles, R.H. *The Book of Jubilees*. In *The Apocrypha and Pseudepigrapha of the Old Testament*. Oxford: Clarendon Press, 1913. Christian Classics Ethereal Library. Online ed. edited by Joshua Williams. https://www.ccel.org/c/charles/pseudepigrapha/jubilee/index.htm.
Dunn, James D. G. *Jesus, Paul, and the Gospels*. Grand Rapids: Eerdmans, 2011.
———. *New Testament Theology: An Introduction*. Nashville: Abingdon, 2009.
Ehrman, Bart D. *The New Testament: A Historical Introduction to Early Christian Writings*. 5th ed. Oxford: Oxford University Press, 2012.
"Gospel of the Nazarenes." Abrahamic Study Hall. https://www.abrahamicstudyhall.org/holy-scriptures/apocryphal/gospel-of-the-nazarenes/. Accessed May 14, 2021.
Hauerwas, Stanley. *Matthew*. London: SCM, 2006.
Hauerwas, Stanley, and William H. Willimon. *The Holy Spirit*. Nashville: Abingdon, 2015.
Hays, Richard B. *Echoes of Scripture in the Gospels*. Waco: Baylor University Press, 2016.
Jewett, Robert. *Romans: A Commentary*. Minneapolis: Fortress, 2007.
Lewis, C. S. *The Silver Chair*. New York: HarperCollins, 1981.

Bibliography

Lincoln, Andrew T. "The Letter to The Colossians." In *The New Interpreter's Bible Commentary* 11, edited by Leander E. Keck, 553-669. Nashville: Abingdon, 2002.

Newbigin, Lesslie. *The Light Has Come: An Exposition of the Fourth Gospel.* Grand Rapids: Eerdmans, 1982.

Noll, Mark A. *Turning Points: Decisive Moments in the History of Christianity.* 3rd ed. Grand Rapids: Baker Academic, 2012.

Rahner, Karl. *The Trinity.* Translated by Joseph Donceel. New York: Herder and Herder, 1970.

Reddish, Mitchell G. *An Introduction to the Gospels.* Nashville: Abingdon, 1997.

Reddish, Tim. *Does God Always Get What God Wants?: An Exploration of God's Activity in a Suffering World.* Eugene, OR: Cascade, 2018.

———. *Science and Christianity: Foundations and Frameworks for Moving Forward in Faith.* Eugene, OR: Wipf & Stock, 2016.

Richardson, Cyril C., ed. and trans. *Didache.* In *Early Christian Fathers.* Vol. 1 of *The Library of Christian Classics.* Philadelphia: Westminster, 1943. Christian Classics Ethereal Library. https://www.ccel.org/ccel/richardson/fathers.viii.i.iii.html.

Sanders, E.P. *The Historical Figure of Jesus.* London: Penguin, 1993.

Wink, Walter. *The Powers that Be: Theology for a New Millennium.* New York: Doubleday, 1998.

Wright, N. T. *The Challenge of Jesus: Rediscovering Who Jesus Was and Is.* Downers Grove, IL: InterVarsity, 1999.

———. *Evil and the Justice of God.* Downers Grove, IL: InterVarsity, 2006.

Wright, N. T., and Michael F. Bird. *The New Testament in Its World: An Introduction to the History, Literature, and Theology of the First Christians.* London: SPCK, 2019.

Yancey, Philip. *The Jesus I Never Knew.* Grand Rapids: Zondervan, 1995.

Other Books by Tim Reddish

DOES GOD ALWAYS GET WHAT GOD WANTS?

An Exploration of God's Activity in a Suffering World

CASCADE BOOKS

"Tim Reddish, trained both in physics and theology, has a nimble mind, and this probing of the relationship between human suffering and God is deft and profound. But mainly this is a deeply personal book, one in which Reddish's own experience with loss and grief sends him farther along the path of faith. His journey takes him not to neatly-crafted answers but instead to the cross of Jesus Christ. Readers of this book will learn much, and they will also be powerfully moved."

THOMAS G. LONG, Bandy Professor of Preaching emeritus, Candler School of Theology, Emory University, and author of *What Shall We Say?: Evil, Suffering, and the Crisis of Faith*

Other Books by Tim Reddish

"Drawing from Scripture, tradition, science, and his own very personal experience with tragedy, Tim Reddish offers readers a clear, comprehensive, and compelling response to the problem of evil—one that doesn't require us to accept that the horrendous suffering people often endure is part of God's grand plan but that nevertheless offers people great hope and comfort. Whether or not readers end up agreeing with every aspect of Reddish's proposal—I do not—they will find a wealth of helpful insights in this powerful book."

GREGORY A. BOYD, Senior Pastor of Woodland Hills Church, St. Paul, Minnesota, and author of *Is God to Blame?* and *Satan and the Problem of Evil*

"Lucid, thought-provoking, insightful, and deeply personal. Reddish shows how the path of suffering can be transformative, even enabling intimacy with our Trinitarian God, who participates in our suffering and with that of all creation. The Trinity's journey of suffering love to the cross can become more profoundly real through our own experiences of pain and brokenness."

FR. RICHARD ROHR, author of *The Divine Dance* and *Job and the Mystery of Suffering*

"Made real and deeply moving by his own experience of life's limits, Tim Reddish has written a thoughtful account of the problem of human suffering and the Christian response to it. This book is well-informed by some of the best treatments of the subject in contemporary literature. It is written in a clear and readable manner, and should serve Christian and non-Christian discussion groups admirably."

DOUGLAS JOHN HALL, Professor of Christian Theology emeritus, McGill University, and author of *God and Human Suffering* and *The Cross in Our Context*

Other Books by Tim Reddish

"Once we set aside belief in a controlling God, faith in God becomes more interesting not less so. Reddish explores the implications in this readable and provocative book. The results create a new vision of God and a way to make sense of suffering and joy."

THOMAS JAY OORD, author of *The Uncontrolling Love of God*.

"A wise, illuminating, and moving book in practical theology—a real pleasure to read."

KEITH WARD, Regius Professor of Divinity emeritus, Oxford, author of *Divine Action* and *Christ and the Cosmos*

"In this little gem of a book, Reddish brings the full weight of his rigorous scientific and theological mind to bear on questions of suffering and God in this world. Grounded in his experience of grief, having suffered the untimely death of his beloved wife, Anne, Reddish examines central doctrines of the faith to consider how they speak *into* the lives of real people living and dying in the here and now. He examines biblical sources, historical and contemporary theology, and especially the theology of the cross to explore questions of theodicy for Christians in today's world. It is an engaging and thoughtful read, written from the heart of a lively and invigorated faith."

PAMELA R. MCCARROLL, Associate Professor of Practical Theology, Emmanuel College, University of Toronto, and author of *Waiting at the Foot of the Cross*

Other Books by Tim Reddish

SCIENCE AND CHRISTIANITY

Foundations and Frameworks for Moving Forward in Faith

WIPF & STOCK

"The polarized positions, from within the church and from skeptics outside, are so loud and so effectively disseminated that it is often difficult for sensible, mediating positions to be heard. But I am encouraged that there are more and more such positions, including this straightforward defense of critical realism. Reddish's concluding challenge to '*Let Scripture be*' should be a helpful word in season for church audiences."

MARK NOLL, Francis A. McAnaney Professor of History at the University of Notre Dame, and author of *Jesus Christ and the Life of the Mind*

"A good book on science and faith needs to be written by someone who has a feel for science from the experience of working it, combined with a depth of theological understanding, and the lightness of touch to make it readable and exciting. Tim Reddish has written this kind of good book."

DAVID WILKINSON, FRAS, Principal of St. John's College, Durham, United Kingdom, and author of *When I Pray What Does God do*?

Other Books by Tim Reddish

"Reddish engages Scripture faithfully and science with professional integrity. In this book readers will find a helpful guide to understanding not just the perennial flash points of science and Christianity, but the deeper issues that have conditioned the modern mind to be suspicious of finding common ground between them. Reddish shows not just that science and faith can get along, but that when each is understood properly, they enrich each other."

JIM STUMP, Senior Editor, *BioLogos*, and author of *Science and Christianity: An Introduction to the Issues*

"This is an informative book of real scholarship in which Tim Reddish addresses the supposed 'conflict' between science and Christianity head-on. By exposing the historical and cultural roots of the divide, he is able to point out where useful dialogue can and should occur."

BILL MCCONKEY, O. Ont, FRSC, Professor emeritus, University of Windsor

"In *Science and Christianity*, Tim Reddish lays an authoritative, yet personal, account of why science and Christianity are not contradictory 'belief systems.' He tackles the big questions that are routinely asked about their relationship—the nature of truth, prayer, the Bible, design in nature, miracles—and offers direct, engaging explanations that will appeal. A great book to read yourself and then give to others."

MIKE HULME, Professor of Climate and Culture, King's College London

Other Books by Tim Reddish

THE AMISH FARMER WHO HATED L.A.

And 8 Other Modern-day Allegories

"In this book the delights of imagination meet timeless stories of Scripture. The outcome is the retelling of deep truths about both the human condition and God's remarkable grace. Tim Reddish has given us a whimsical and thought-provoking read that is also pure pleasure."

Rev. Dr. Judy Paulsen, Professor of Evangelism, Wycliffe College, Toronto

"Tim Reddish writes to address difficult questions from interesting angles. His work feels fresh, contemporary, challenging, and thought-provoking—without departing from orthodox faith. This book helps us to reflect on our lives, the better to serve the One who gave us life."

Ven. Nick Barker, Archdeacon of Auckland and Priest-in-Charge of Holy Trinity, Darlington, United Kingdom

Other Books by Tim Reddish

"This collection of short stories warms the heart and provides insight into how God is at work through people today. The stories take biblical topics and situate them into contemporary cultural settings, and so help to open our eyes to their meaning for today. Tim Reddish takes on a number of interesting topics and handles them with grace."

Dr. John Sanders, Professor of Religious Studies, Hendrix College, and author of *The God Who Risks*

"In reading each of Tim's stories I had an '*Aha!*' moment when I realized which familiar Bible story he was depicting, only to discover an unexpected twist around the next corner. These stories are full of gentle humor and great insight which will keep the reader thinking for days after reading them."

Rev. Dr. Stuart Macdonald, Professor of Church and Society, Knox College, Toronto

www.ingramcontent.com/pod-product-compliance
Lightning Source LLC
Chambersburg PA
CBHW070930160426
43193CB00011B/1639